THE KIDS' BOOK OF 6 AWESOME ACTIVITIES

By
Tony Tallarico

kids books
Incorporated

Hours of challenging fun and games are in store for you in

THE KIDS' BOOK OF AWESOME ACTIVITIES.

Each book is chock full of secret codes, mazes, hidden picture puzzles, word finds, riddles, crosswords, things to draw, and many other zany activities. There's never a dull moment, so get ready to have a blast as you test your skills trying to solve these awesome puzzles.

What are you waiting for? Sharpen your pencil and let's go!

Answers begin on page 158.

Which One's Different?

Three of the four robots below are exactly the same. Circle the one that is different.

These two cowboys look the same. Or do they?
Find and circle at least 10 things that make
them different.

What's Wrong Here?
Find and circle all the things you find wrong with this picture.

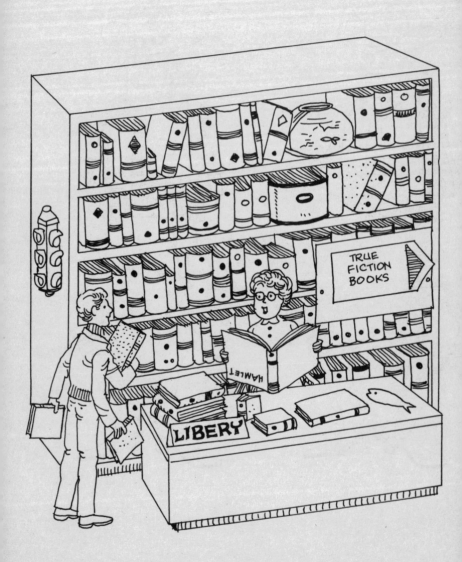

These friendly martians need to return to their flying saucer. You can help them by finding the path of numbers that add up to **21**.

Travel through this maze by spelling:

SPACE EXPLORER.

These scouts have lost their space rocket.
Guide them back to it by following the path
of triangles only.

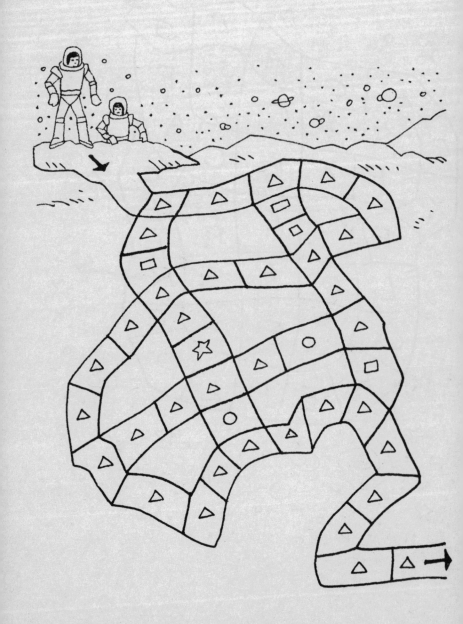

CROSSWORD FUN

In the puzzle below, think of a word for each numbered clue, going across or down, and put the letters of the word in the diagram.

Across
3. A tank to swim in.
5. First day of the week.
6. Twelve minus four.
7. Not a lie.

Down
1. _____ and Dad.
2. Nine plus two.
4. A spring month.
5. Not sour.

NIAGARA FALLS VACATION

This natural wonder flows from Lake Erie into Lake Ontario and attracts tourists from all over to view it.
Can you find the following hidden objects in the Falls?

• FISH • KEY • BOTTLE • STAR • FLOWER •
• BASEBALL • RING • TRIANGLE • APPLE •

SNAPSHOT SOUVENIRS

Taking photographs is a great way to remember the fun you've had on your vacation.
How many times does the word CAMERA appear below?
Circle and count each one. Write the total below.

```
C   A   R   E   M   A   C

C   A   M   E   R   A   A

A   R   C   R   M   R   M

M   E   A   E   E   R   E

E   M   R   M   M   C   R

R   A   A   R   C   M   A

A   C   A   M   E   R   A
```

_____

TOTAL

WISH YOU WERE HERE

Don't you wish you could take all your friends with you on vacation? Use this chart to decode this special message.

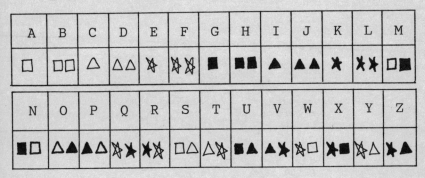

A	B	C	D	E	F	G	H	I	J	K	L	M
□	□□	△	△△	✻	✻✻	■	■■	▲	▲▲	✶	✶✶	□■

N	O	P	Q	R	S	T	U	V	W	X	Y	Z
■□	△▲	▲△	△✶	✻✶	□△	△✻	■▲	▲✻	✻□	✶■	✻△	✶▲

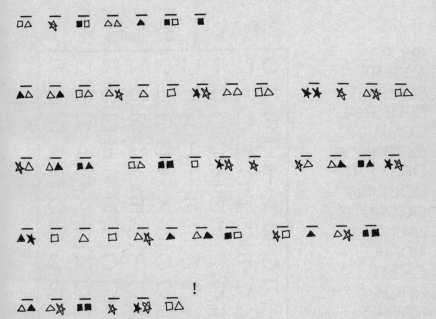

SENDING POSTCARDS LETS YOU SHARE YOUR VACATION WITH OTHERS!

In the following word-search puzzles, find and circle the words from the lists below. They can be found in straight lines going FORWARD, BACKWARD, UP, DOWN, or DIAGONALLY.

SPACE TALK

ABORT
ASCENT
BURNOUT
CELESTIAL
COMMAND
CORRIDOR
DESCENT
DOCKING
GUIDANCE
LAUNCH
MODULE
ORBIT
PITCH
RADAR
RETROROCKET
ROLL
YAW

```
O L T U O N R U B
R A E L U D O M T
B U G A G E D R E
I N U I N S I A K
T C I T I C R D C
A H D S K E R A O
B C A E C N O R R
O P N L O T C N O
R U C E D L L O R
T N E C S A B D T
C O M M A N D C E
P I T C H Y A W R
```

MOVING DAY

BEDS
BOOKS
BOXES
BROOM
CHAIRS
CHINA
CLOTHES
COUCH
CURTAINS
DESK
FURNITURE
LAMPS
MOPS
PANS
PIANO
PICTURES
POTS
RECORD
RUGS
TOYS

```
B E D S M O O R B
O O U X H C U O C
O M X T S Y O T U
K P R E C O R D R
S P A N S P O M T
R R F S U I L K A
I D E S K A A R I
A N I H C N M U N
H G H S T O P G S
C L O T H E S S V
T P I C T U R E S
E R U T I N R U F
```

SUMMER

BEACH
BICYCLING
CAMP
HIKING
HOTDOGS
LEMONADE
PICNICS
POOL
SHORTS
SUN
SUNBURN
SUNTAN
SWIM

```
X T H C A E B T V
S H O R T S I U S
W U T R C N C L U
I P D F T C Y E N
M N O S T O C M B
G P G A A A L O U
Y L S A M T I N R
L O O P F N N A N
P H I K I N G D S
V A C A T I Y E U
U P I C N I C S N
N S S U N T A N R
```

... Another Word-Search Puzzle

BREAKFAST

BACON
BUTTER
COCOA
COFFEE
CREAM
EGGS
GRAPEFRUIT
HAM
JAM
JELLY
JUICE
MILK
MUFFIN
OATMEAL
ORANGE
ROLL
TEA
TOAST

```
M O G J U I C E B
U A R K G L I A B
F T A O C O C U H
F M P B M O T F A
I E E P N T T U M
N A F E E F F O C
E L R R L G B Y R
G T U N C M G J E
N S I F U I E S A
A A T E A L J A M
R O A C L K K L N
O T B Y R O L L U
```

THINGS THAT GO TOGETHER

SPRING IS THE TIME FOR PLANTING. THIS SCARE-
CROW WILL KEEP THE BIRDS AWAY FROM THE SEEDS.
THERE ARE 9 BIRDS HIDDEN IN THIS PICTURE. CAN
YOU FIND THEM?

FIND AND CIRCLE THE TWO FLOWER ARRANGEMENTS THAT ARE EXACTLY THE SAME.

FLYING A KITE

The four kids below are flying their kites, but one kite is about to get away. Can you figure out whose kite it is?

Coded Jokes and Riddles

For a real laugh, use the chart to match codes with letters. Write the letters in the blanks provided above the coded jokes and riddles.

SUN	MON	TUE	WED	THU	FRI	SAT
	1 L	2 N	3 H	4 B	5 Q	6 K
7 F	8 R	9 C	10 V	11 P	12 Z	13 E
14 A	15 M	16 U	17 G	18 W	19 J	20 X
21 I	22 T	23 O	24 Y	25 S	26 D	

THU WED SUN MON   SUN THU
18   3   14 22   21 25

SUN   THU TUE MON MON
14   4   16   1   1

TUE SUN MON MON SAT FRI
9   14   1   1   13 26

THU WED SAT TUE
18   3   13   2

WED SAT ' THU
3   13   25

THU MON SAT SAT THU SUN TUE WED   ?
25   1   13 13 11 21   2   17

SUN
14

THU TUE MON MON FRI TUE FRI SAT MON   !
4   16   1   1   26 23 12 13   8

WHAT GOES UP INTO THE AIR
WHITE AND COMES DOWN YELLOW
AND WHITE?

$\overline{\text{SUN}}$ $\overline{\text{TUE}}$ $\overline{\text{SAT}}$ $\overline{\text{WED}}$ $\overline{\text{WED}}$!
14   2   13   17   17

WHAT DO YOU GET WHEN YOU
CROSS A KANGAROO WITH A
747 JET?

$\overline{\text{SUN}}$ $\overline{\text{THU}}$ $\overline{\text{MON}}$ $\overline{\text{SUN}}$ $\overline{\text{TUE}}$ $\overline{\text{SAT}}$
14   11   1   14   2   13

$\overline{\text{MON}}$ $\overline{\text{WED}}$ $\overline{\text{SUN}}$ $\overline{\text{MON}}$
22   3   14   22

$\overline{\text{MON}}$ $\overline{\text{SUN}}$ $\overline{\text{SAT}}$ $\overline{\text{SAT}}$ $\overline{\text{THU}}$
15   14   6   13   25

$\overline{\text{THU}}$ $\overline{\text{WED}}$ $\overline{\text{TUE}}$ $\overline{\text{MON}}$ $\overline{\text{MON}}$
25   3   23   8   22

$\overline{\text{WED}}$ $\overline{\text{TUE}}$ $\overline{\text{THU}}$ $\overline{\text{THU}}$!
3   23   11   25

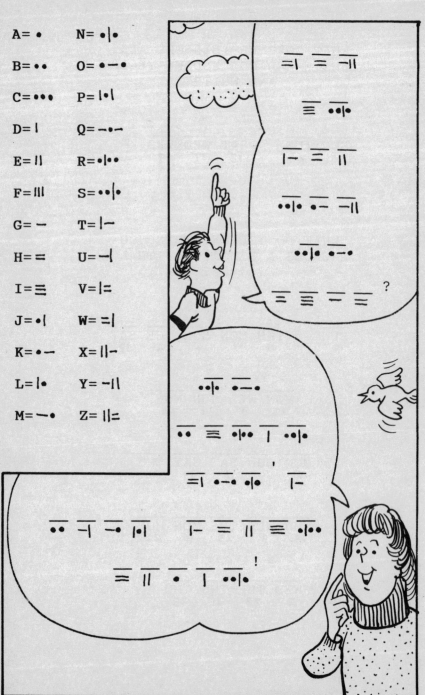

A = •   N = •|•

B = ••   O = •—•

C = ••• P = |•|

D = | Q = —•—

E = || R = •|••

F = ||| S = ••|•

G = —   T = |—

H = =   U = —|

I = ≡   V = |=

J = •| W = =|

K = •—   X = ||—

L = |•   Y = —||

M = —•   Z = ||=

"IF YOU SHOVELED SNOW FOR 25
PEOPLE AND THEY EACH PAID
YOU FOUR DOLLARS, WHAT
WOULD YOU GET?"

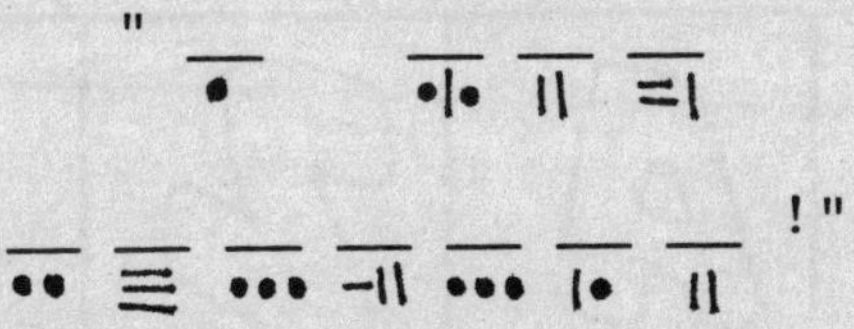

"IS THIS THE END OF THE LINE?"

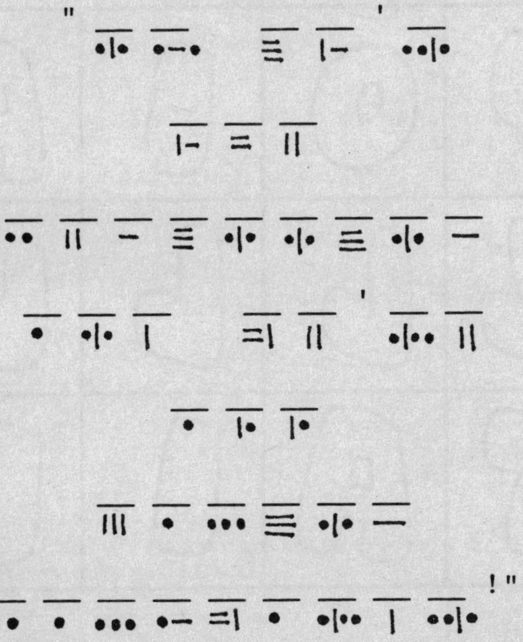

TO FORM THIS PHRASE, CROSS OUT ALL THE LETTERS THAT APPEAR **3** TIMES ONLY. WRITE THE REMAINING LETTERS, AS THEY APPEAR, IN THE BLANKS BELOW.

D	A	Z	O
I	N	T	Z
P	O	I	A
Z	L	L	U
T	A	I	E

_ _ _ ' _

_ _ _ _ _ _ _ !

28

USE THIS CHART TO DECODE THE MESSAGE.

A	B	C	D	E	F	G	H	I	J	K	L	M
13	5	17	6	20	24	12	10	26	3	14	7	23

N	O	P	Q	R	S	T	U	V	W	X	Y	Z
16	8	25	2	22	11	18	4	21	19	9	15	1

___ ___ ___ ___
6   8   12   11

___ ___ ___
13   16   6

___ ___ ___ ___
17   13   18   11

___ ___ ___ ___
16   20   20   6

___ ___ ___ ___
7   8   21   20

___ ___ ___
13   16   6

___ ___ ___ ___ .
17   13   22   20

COMPLETE THE CROSSWORD PUZZLE. WRITE AND UNSCRAMBLE THE CIRCLED LETTERS BELOW TO MAKE THE NAME OF A COUNTRY.

• ACROSS

2- OPPOSITE OF WEST.

3- DAYTIME MEAL.

5- MONTH AFTER AUGUST.

• DOWN

1- OPPOSITE OF STAND.

2- NOT LATE.

4- _ _ _ _ -AND- SEEK.

5- DOG, CAT, BIRD, RABBIT, ETC.

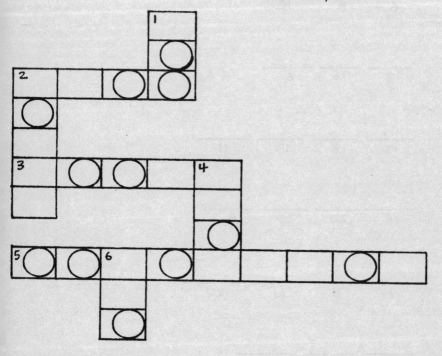

‾ ‾ ‾ ‾ ‾ ‾ ‾ ‾ ‾ ‾ ‾ ‾
SCRAMBLED CIRCLED LETTERS

‾ ‾ ‾ ‾ ‾ ‾ ‾ ‾ ‾ ‾ ‾ ‾
UNSCRAMBLED NAME OF A COUNTRY - 2 WORDS

LET'S GO ON A SPACE TRIP.

Find the following objects in this design:
STAR • HAT • HEART • KEY • PEN • SCISSORS •
CANDLE • CUPCAKE • APPLE • PEAR • KITE

Find and outline the 8 stars hidden below.

How many things can you find wrong with this disco scene?

Double-Trouble Riddle Fun!

In the following Double-Trouble puzzles,
unscramble the underlined word in each riddle.
Then place it in the crossword puzzle.

ACROSS

1. Why are wolves like playing cards?
They always come in APKCS.

4. Who would never live in Grant's Tomb?
General ARNTG.

5. Why does an ox always smile when it's working?
It's got a OKEY on its mind.

7. When does a book change color?
When it's DEAR.

9. Why does a spider spin its web?
Because it doesn't know how to IKNT.

DOWN

1. Which tattle-tale animal always squeals on you?
GPI.

2. What are the world's strongest coughing birds?
The whooping CARSNE.

3. Who would you hire to set your table in London?
An English ESTERT.

6. What do you put on a sick pig?
KOINment.

8. Why can't you sneak up on a cornstalk?
It's loaded with AESR.

. . . Another Double-Trouble Puzzle

ACROSS

3. Why is that man driving his boat so fast?
   The guy on AWTRE skis is chasing him.

5. Where does baby corn come from?
   The ASTLK brings it.

6. What would you say if I told you my bed
   was a mile wide?
   That's a lot of BNKU.

8. Which country is incorporated?
   India KIN.

9. How can you tell if a man from Brussels
   has an upset stomach?
   Ask him if he's BELNAIG.

DOWN

1. Why does the Statue of Liberty stand in
   New York harbor?
   It can't IST down.

2. What prize did the broom win in the contest?
   The WPSEE stakes.

4. Why are moths always hungry?
   They only AET holes.

5. What's different about a mathematician's plant?
   It grows SAEQUR roots.

MILE

7. Who can never be the
   Queen of England?
   The GKIN.

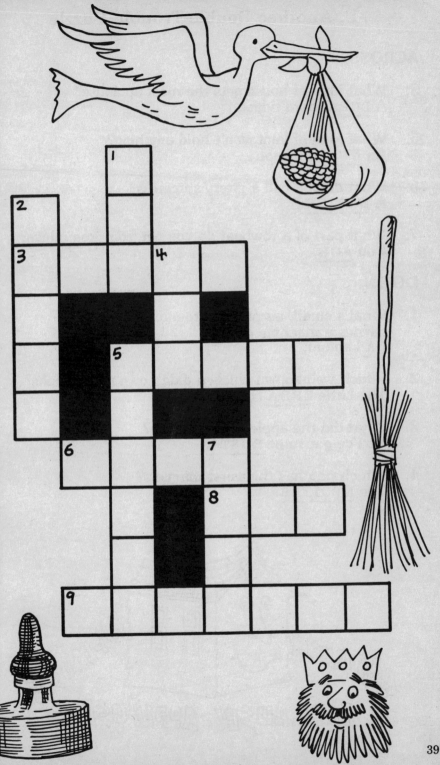

... **Another Double-Trouble Puzzle**

ACROSS

3. What kind of house gets the most applause?
   A LCPA board house.

5. What kind of knot won't hold anything?
   An NUEDIT knot.

6. What do you call a jittery sorceress?
   A WTTICH.

7. What part of a rowboat do you get from iron mines?
   Iron AOR.

DOWN

1. What's small, purple, and round, and
   carries a machine gun?
   LA kaplum.

2. Which well-known chicken didn't own many books?
   The Little ERDA Hen.

3. What did the apple say to the pie?
   You've got some RUSTC.

4. Which dog has the worst manners?
   The NPOITER.

40

. . . Another Double-Trouble Puzzle

ACROSS

1. What did the cotton plant say to the farmer?
   Stop <u>IIPKGNC</u> on me.

4. What is the dirtiest word in the world?
   <u>OOPLLUTIN</u>.

6. What happens to naughty pigs?
   They are made into <u>VDEILED</u> ham.

DOWN

1. What do you get if you cross a dog with
   a chicken?
   <u>POODCHE</u> eggs on toast.

2. What do hunters catch easiest in winter?
   A bad <u>LCOD</u>.

3. Which floor of a department store has spooks?
   The <u>OGHST</u> story.

5. What is the only thing you should put in an eye?
   A piece of <u>HTREDA</u>.

ARF!

DO NOT
WAKE
THE
GHOSTS

44

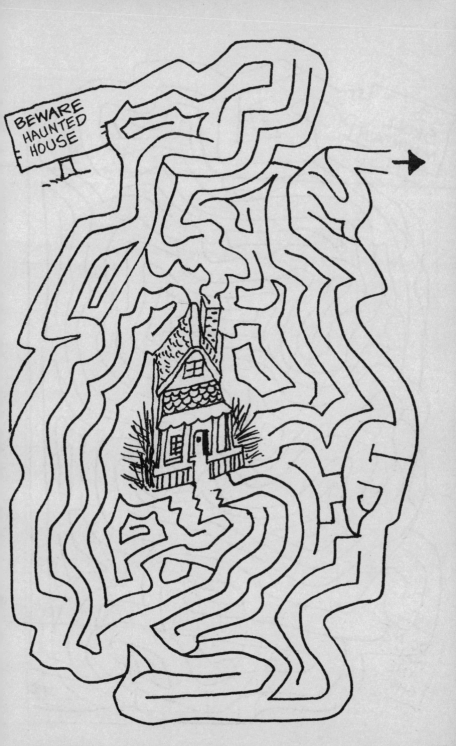

TO
SKULL
MOUNTAIN

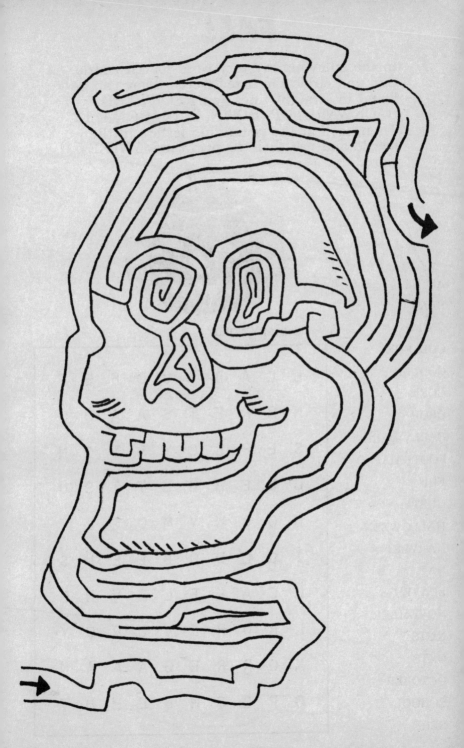

FALL

In the following mystery word-search puzzle, find and circle the listed words. They can be found in straight lines going FORWARD, BACKWARD, UP, DOWN, or DIAGONALLY. Then, look at the remaining letters in the puzzle and use them to form the MYSTERY word.

ASTER

BARN

CHILL

COLLEGE

COOLER

CORN

CROP

EARLY DARK

FOOTBALL

FUN

GUSTY

HALLOWEEN

HARVEST

HAY

LEAVES

NOVEMBER

NUTS

OATS

OCTOBER

SCHOOL

SERE

MYSTERY WORD __ __ __ __ __ __

L	L	A	B	T	O	O	F	E	F
N	R	R	E	T	S	A	A	U	O
S	E	R	E	C	Y	R	T	C	N
C	L	E	H	B	L	T	T	S	U
H	O	O	W	Y	M	O	S	L	T
I	O	L	D	O	B	E	E	U	S
L	C	A	L	E	L	A	V	N	G
L	R	O	R	E	V	L	R	O	Y
K	O	R	R	E	G	A	A	A	N
O	P	S	S	N	B	E	H	H	T

48

... Another Mystery Word-Search Puzzle

SUMMER

"In the good old summertime," when "the livin' is easy," we enjoy vacations and rest, but complain about heat, bugs and sunburn. Find the joys and everyday facts of summer in this puzzle.

ANTS
AUGUST
BANG
BEACH
BIKINI

CAMPFIRE
CANNER
CANOE
DREAM
HALTER
HEAT
ICE
JULY FOURTH
JUNE
NATURE
PLAYS
SHADY
SIP
SUN
SUNBURN
SWIM
TAN
TORRID
TRUNKS
WARM
WATER
WET

MYSTERY WORD ___ ___ ___

```
T E W Y D A H S U N
M R A W R I T E A H
I I T O E N R T A E
W N E T A E U R R T
S I R S M R O I O R
H K E U E S F N E T
C I N G B P Y T A E
A B N U M N L A N C
E A A A R A U U L T
B E C I H T J S I P
```

Link-Up Puzzle

Place the words in the diagram so that all fit perfectly.

4 letter words	7 letter words	8 letter words
CARE	DESTROY	OBSOLETE
GONE		WILDLIFE
HELP		
HOPE		

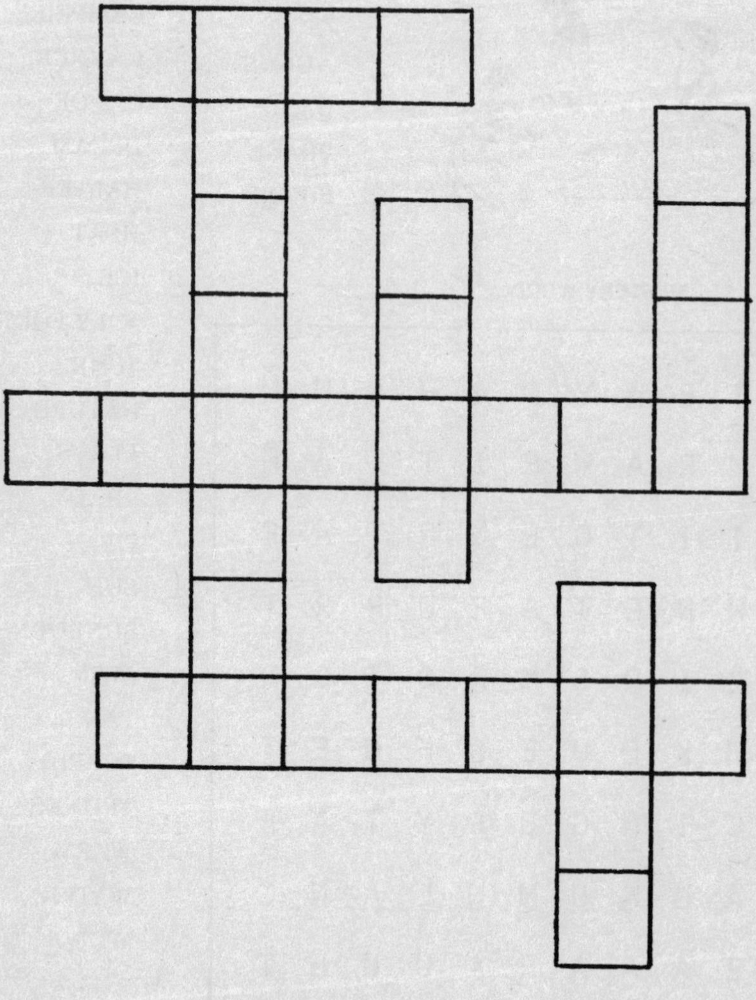

Unscramble these words having to do with animals and place the numbered letters in their correct spaces below.

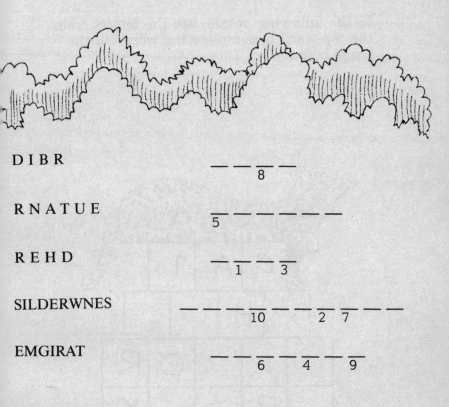

D I B R

— — —₈ —

R N A T U E

—₅ — — — — —

R E H D

— —₁ —₃ —

SILDERWNES

— — — —₁₀ — —₂ —₇ — — —

EMGIRAT

— — —₆ — —₄ — —₉

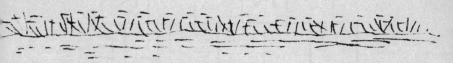

—₁ —₂ —₃ —₄ —₅ —₆ —₇ —₈ —₉ —₁₀

Leopards are at home in the tropical forests, open plains, and mountains of Asia and Africa. These 100-pound cats have long been hunted for their beautiful skins.

In the following puzzle, use the letters from the top word to complete the words in the boxes below.

At one time, Prezwalski's Horse, was seen throughout Central Asia. The last of the wild horses, the species gets its name from the Russian explorer who discovered them in 1881.

To discover where they survive today, circle the letters that contain an even number. List these letters in the spaces below.

⁵T	²M	¹¹D	³H
⁷L	¹⁵W	⁸O	¹B
⁴N	²¹E	⁵K	¹⁰G
¹R	¹²O	¹⁸L	⁷V
⁶I	³Y	⁹G	²A

SOUTHWESTERN __ __ __ __ __ __ __ __
          2 8 4 10 12 18 6 2

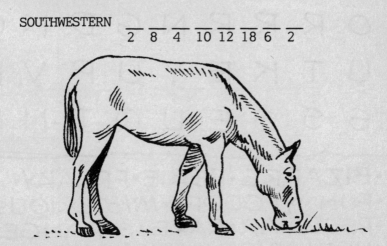

THAT'S ODD

In the following word-search puzzles, find and circle the words from the lists below. They can be found in straight lines going FORWARD, BACKWARD, UP, DOWN, or DIAGONALLY.

```
M R A I L U C E P
Y T T I W E I R D
S V E R R A Z I B
T E Z F R E A K Y
E G O O F Y W Q N
R N C E U Y I O N
I A D I N L L O A
O R R R N G D K C
U T K E Y U P V N
S S S E U Q I N U
```

• BIZARRE • EERIE • FREAKY •
• FUNNY • GOOFY • MYSTERIOUS •
• PECULIAR • RARE • STRANGE •
• UGLY • UNCANNY • UNIQUE •
• WEIRD • WILD • WITTY •

BE A CLOWN

```
L Z C I T N A D P
U P I R T C J L R
F L P U E K A M O
R C O S T U M E P
O E O W G R I N S
L T A H O T U I Y
O P C F S H S T N
C I R C U S S U N
Z E L I M S O O U
P L D F N W O R F
```

•ACT •ANTIC •CIRCUS •
•COLORFUL •COSTUME •
•FROWN •FUNNY •GRIN •HAT •
•LAUGH •MAKE-UP •PERFORM •
•PROPS •ROUTINE •SHOW •SMILE •
•TRIP •

. . . Another Word-Search Puzzle

WEIRD THINGS TO KEEP IN A CAR

```
C E M E N T J G M
F L A T T I R E I
R B U E S E E H C
O A M V P C T O R
G T T R V Y S D O
S N N A A S A S W
Y R B R A F O L A
X U N L E A T Y V
T T Z F P V C N E
V M U I R A U Q A
```

•ANT FARM •AQUARIUM•
•CEMENT•CHEESE•FLAT TIRE•
•FROGS•LASSO•MICROWAVE•
•SOAP•TOASTER•TUBA•
•TURNTABLE•YARN•

WACKY SOUNDING "X" WORDS

```
L V Y S I X A X X
S O X Y L A N E E
M E L Y X O R R N
S N G Y N D C O O
C I R E X I E S L
C H X Y H S G E I
E T M T O N C R T
B N N L Y C Y E H
E A Y A I N E X L
X X Y S T E R L E
```

•XANTHIC •XANTHINE •XAXIS•
•XEBEC •XENIA •XENOLITH•
•XENON •XERIC •XERD•
•XEROSERE •XYLAN •XYLEM•
•XYLOL •XYLOSE •XYSTER•

A Mystery Picture To Draw

Can you guess what this mystery picture is? To find out, draw exactly what you see in the numbered boxes at the top of the page into the blank boxes of the same number below.

1	2	3	4
5	6	7	8
9	10	11	12
13	14	15	16

... Another Mystery Picture To Draw

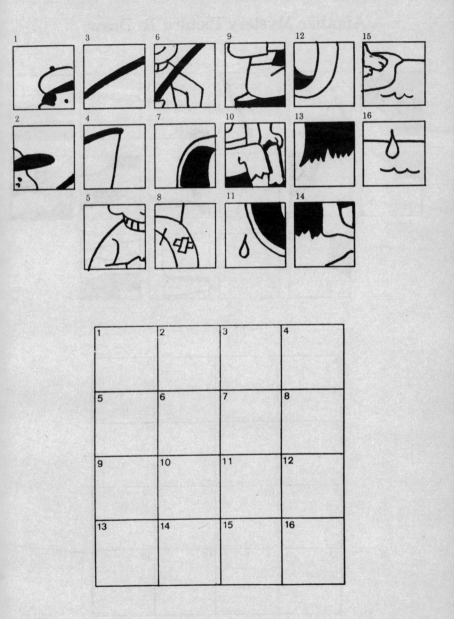

. . . Another Mystery Picture To Draw

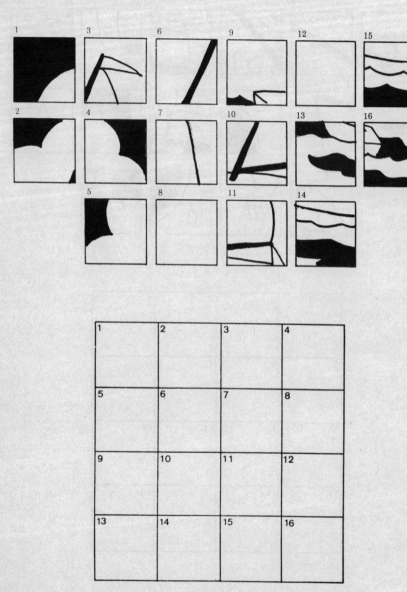

... Another Mystery Picture To Draw

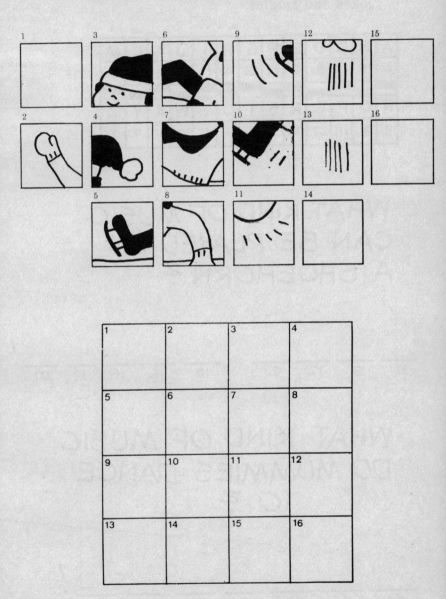

Coded Jokes and Riddles

Use the chart to match code numbers with letters. Then, write the letters in the blanks provided, and you'll get the answers to the jokes and riddles.

A	B	C	D	E	F	G	H	I	J	K	L	M
6	15	20	8	2	19	23	14	17	24	4	12	10

N	O	P	Q	R	S	T	U	V	W	X	Y	Z
9	3	18	22	26	11	5	16	25	13	21	7	1

WHAT KIND OF MUSIC CAN BE PLAYED ON A SHOEHORN?

___ ___ ___ ___   ___ ___ ___ ___ ___ !
11   3 12   2   10 16 11 17 20

WHAT KIND OF MUSIC DO MUMMIES DANCE TO?

___ ___ ___ ___ ___ ___ ___ !
26   6 23   5 17 10   2

WHAT KIND OF PETS MAKE MUSIC?

___ ___ ___ ___ ___ ___ ___ ___ !
5 26 16 10 18 2 5 11

WHICH FISH ARE THE BEST SINGERS ?

___ ___ ___ ___ !
15 6 11 11

WHAT CAN'T BE BEATEN ?

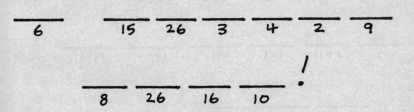

___   ___ ___ ___ ___ ___ ___
6   15 26 3 4 2 9

___ ___ ___ ___ !
8 26 16 10

A	B	C	D	E	F	G
•	••	•••	|	||	|||	•|

H	I	J	K	L	M	N
••|	•••|	|•	|••	|•••	•||	||•

O	P	Q	R	S	T	U
|•|	||•||	|••	•|•	•||•	|||•	•|||

V	W	X	Y	Z
•|•••	••|•	•||••	••||•	|||•|||

WHAT IS A MONSTER'S FAVORITE HOLIDAY?

_____   _____   _____   _____   _____
 •   \|\|•\|\| •\|• •••\| \|•••

_____ _____ _____ _____ _____ _____ '
 •\| ••\| \|•\| •\|\|\| \|••• •\|\|•

_____ _____ _____ !
 \| •   ••\|\|•

WHAT HAS TEETH BUT CAN'T EAT?

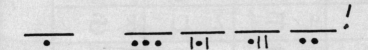

WHERE WAS THE SPACE CREATURE WHEN THE LIGHTS WENT OUT?

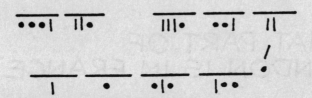

WHAT DOES THE MONTH OF DECEMBER HAVE THAT NO OTHER MONTH HAS?

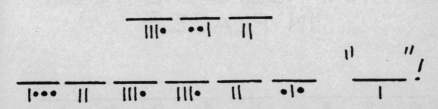

⭘		⬜		△		✶	
1	D	8	O	1	J	7	B
2	L	9	F	2	U	8	S
3	G	10	P	3	I	9	M
4	T	11	A	4	R	10	E
5	N	12	Q	5	V	11	W
6	K	13	H	6	Z	12	Y
7	C	14	X				

WHAT PART OF LONDON IS IN FRANCE?

$$\frac{}{\overset{⭘}{4}} \quad \frac{}{\overset{⬜}{13}} \quad \frac{}{\overset{✶}{10}}$$

$$\frac{}{\overset{⭘}{2}} \quad \frac{}{\overset{✶}{10}} \quad \frac{}{\overset{⭘}{4}} \quad \frac{}{\overset{⭘}{4}} \quad \frac{}{\overset{✶}{10}} \quad \frac{}{\overset{△}{4}} \quad {}^{''}\frac{}{\overset{⭘}{5}}{}^{''}!$$

WHAT KEEPS THE MOON IN PLACE?

$$\frac{}{\overset{△}{3}} \quad \frac{}{\overset{⭘}{4}} \quad \frac{}{\overset{✶}{8}} \qquad \frac{}{\overset{✶}{7}} \quad \frac{}{\overset{✶}{10}} \quad \frac{}{\overset{⬜}{11}} \quad \frac{}{\overset{✶}{9}} \quad \frac{}{\overset{✶}{8}}!$$

WHAT PLANT HAS THE MOST MONEY?

___ ___ ___ ___ !
✿9 △3 ○5 ○4

WHEN DID THE MILK BLUSH?

___ ___ ___ ___   ___ ___
✿11 □13 ✿10 ○5   △3 ○4

___ ___ ___   ___ ___ ___
✿8 □11 ✿11   ○4 □13 ✿10

___ ___ ___ ___ ___
✿8 □11 ○2 □11 ○1

___ ___ ___ ___ ___ ___ ___ ___ !
○1 △4 ✿10 ✿8 ✿8 △3 ○5 ○3

WHAT CAT IS FUZZY AND LOOKS LIKE A WORM?

___ ___ ___ ___ ___ ___ ___ ___ ___ ___ !
○7 □11 ○4 ✿10 △4 □10 △3 ○2 ○2 □11 △4

A	B	C	D	E	F	G	H	I
x	xx	xxx	xxxx	o	oo	ooo	oooo	xo

J	K	L	M	N	O	P	Q	R
xxo	xxxo	xxxxo	ox	oox	ooox	oooox	xox	xoox

S	T	U	V	W	X	Y	Z	
oxo	oxxo	xoxo	oxox	xxoo	ooxx	xoo	xxxooo	

WHY ARE ELEPHANTS SO POOR?

___ ___ ___ ___ ___ ___ ___
xx   o   xxx   x   xoxo   oxo   o

___ ___ ___ ___   ___ ___ ___ ___
oxxo oooo o xoo   xxoo ooox xoox xxxo

___ ___ ___
oo ooox xoox

___ ___ ___ ___ ___ ___ ___ !
oooox o x oox xoxo oxxo oxo

WHERE CAN HAPPINESS AND MONEY BE FOUND?

___ ___ ___ ___ ___ ___ ___ ___ ___ !
xxxx xo xxx oxxo xo ooox oox x xoox xoo

WHAT DO SNOWMEN PUT IN THEIR SALAD?

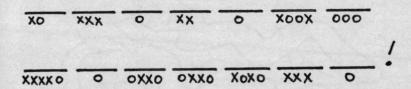

```
___   ___   ___   ___   ___   ___   ___
 XO   XXX    O    XX     O   XOOX  OOO
```

```
____   ___   ___   ___   ___   ___   ___   !
XXXXO    O   OXXO  OXXO  XOXO  XXX    O
```

WHY CAN A HAMBURGER RUN A MILE IN UNDER THREE MINUTES?

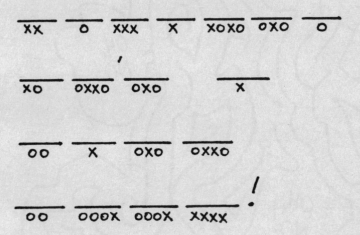

```
___   ___   ___   ___   ___   ___   ___
 XX    O    XXX    X   XOXO  OXO    O
```

```
                     '
___   ___   ___          ___
 XO   OXXO  OXO           X
```

```
___   ___   ___   ___
 OO    X    OXO  OXXO
```

```
___   ___   ___   ___   !
 OO  OOOX  OOOX  XXXX
```

WHAT DO YOU CALL A SKELETON WITH NO BRAINS?

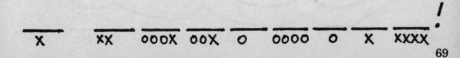

```
___   ___   ___   ___   ___   ___   ___   ___   ___   !
 X     XX  OOOX  OOX    O   OOOO   O    X   XXXX
```

There's a full moon out! If you're lucky in this maze, you'll meet up with a werewolf who likes to eat hamburgers.

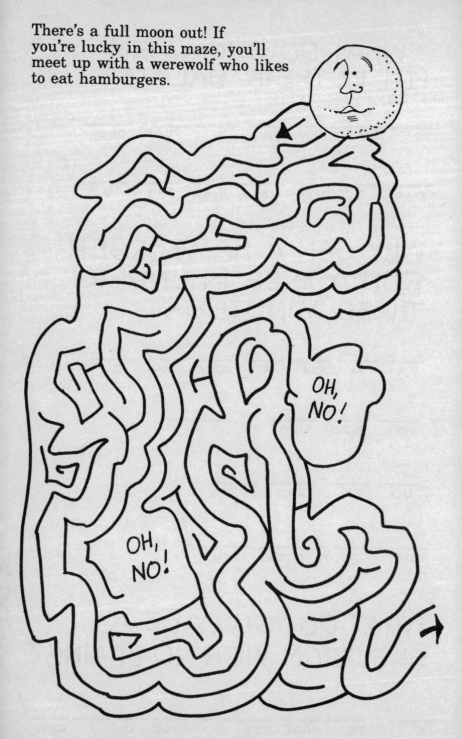

YOU MADE IT SAFELY THROUGH!

On the opposite page, complete the dot-to-dot and you'll find out what's scaring the diver. Then, help the diver reach land by guiding him through the maze below.

Find and circle the 2 sand sharks that are exactly the same

Find and circle the 2 perlon sharks that are exactly the same.

U.F.O.'s?

In the following word-search puzzles, find and circle the words from the lists below. They can be found in straight lines going FORWARD, BACKWARD, UP, DOWN, or DIAGONALLY.

```
E V G A L A X Y T S
D E R U T A E R C J
A J G N A I T R A M
V P I H S E C A P S
N N V N K V H D T A
I W U C Y Y A E U U
C O O G E E S Y R C
I R O R Y E E E E E
G Z A P L A N E T R
A M O O N D R N U S
M A R S R E W O P O
```

•CAPTURE•CHASE•CREATURE•
•GALAXY•INVADE•MAGIC•
•MARS•MARTIAN•MOON•
•ONE EYED•PLANET•POWERS•
•RAY GUN•ROCKET•SAUCER•
•SPACESHIP•SUN•WORLD•
•ZAP•

YOU PUT PEANUT BUTTER ON WHAT?!!

```
T R U G O Y Z U B
C A R R O T S W P
H S L A E M T A O
E G T P Y F N T B
R I G E I C P E C
R F S S A D E R N
I V H K A K A M R
E N E L A E R E C
S S A T D V S L L
O S E O T A T O P
I L O I V A R N C
```

•CARROTS •CEREAL•
•CHERRIES •FIGS •FISH•
•GRAPES •OATMEAL•
•PANCAKES •PEARS•
•POTATOES •RAVIOLI•
•SALAD •STEAK•
•WATERMELON •YOGURT•

30 WACKY THINGS TO BRING TO THE BEACH

```
L A U N D R Y D K
A A F O S P E O I
U F F I I S E N T
N U Y T K L P A C
F R A C S M B I H
R C R E A R L P E
Y O E L E H U S N
I A T L I C B E T
N T U O T R T T A
G R P C W A H A B
P E M P O T G K L
A D O M B S I S E
N D C A N D L E S
C A Z T N L D C D
S L Y S A N D I C
```

• BOW TIE • CANDLES • COMPUTER • DESK •
• FRYING PAN • FUR COAT • ICE SKATES •
• KITCHEN TABLE • LADDER • LAMP • LAUNDRY •
• LIGHT BULB • OIL • PIANO • RULER • SAND •
• SCARF • SOFA • STAMP COLLECTION • STARCH •

WACKY PLACES TO HIDE
MONEY

```
A P R E Z E E R F
P I Z Z A P I E A
R O O F L Z Z F D
E G A R A G A R C
C A K E M S U I O
O O L G I M T G F
R I D T N T O E F
D N E A A N O R E
S X B P D E L A E
L O R P E M B T C
E B E L F E O O A
E L D E F S X R N
V I N P U A P B R
E A U I T B O O K
V M T E S O L C O
```

• APPLE PIE • ATTIC • BASEMENT • BOOK •
• CAKE • CLOSET • COFFEE CAN • DRUM •
• FREEZER • IGLOO • GARAGE • MAILBOX •
• PIZZA PIE • RECORD SLEEVE •
• REFRIGERATOR • ROOF • STUFFED ANIMAL •
• TOOL BOX • UNDER BED •

How many things can you find wrong
in this picture? Circle them.

Which backpack is different from the others? Find and circle it.

Unscramble these words having to do with school.

O B K O   — — — —

R D E A   — — — —

S L A C S   — — — — —

U B S   — — —

Y L A P   — — — —

N R A E L   — — — — —

What can you always expect teachers to give to students? Cross out every **THIRD LETTER** and list the remaining letters, as they appear, in the spaces below.

— — — — — — —

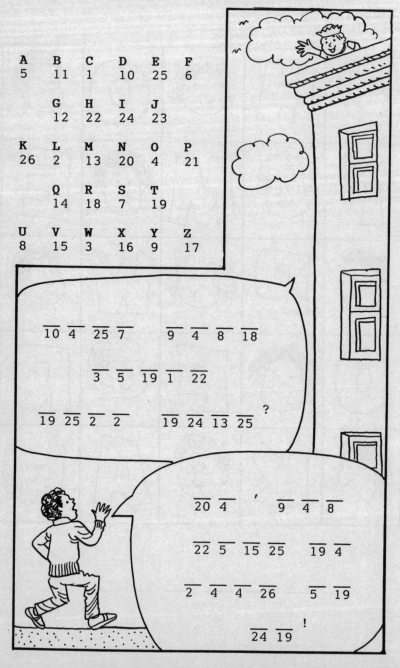

Coded Jokes and Riddles

Use the chart to match code numbers with letters. Write the letters in the blanks provided above the coded jokes and riddles.

A	B	C	D	E	F
5	11	1	10	25	6

	G	H	I	J
	12	22	24	23

K	L	M	N	O	P
26	2	13	20	4	21

	Q	R	S	T
	14	18	7	19

U	V	W	X	Y	Z
8	15	3	16	9	17

$\overline{10}\ \overline{4}\ \overline{25}\ \overline{7}\qquad \overline{9}\ \overline{4}\ \overline{8}\ \overline{18}$

$\overline{3}\ \overline{5}\ \overline{19}\ \overline{1}\ \overline{22}$

$\overline{19}\ \overline{25}\ \overline{2}\ \overline{2}\qquad \overline{19}\ \overline{24}\ \overline{13}\ \overline{25}$?

$\overline{20}\ \overline{4}\qquad ,\qquad \overline{9}\ \overline{4}\ \overline{8}$

$\overline{22}\ \overline{5}\ \overline{15}\ \overline{25}\qquad \overline{19}\ \overline{4}$

$\overline{2}\ \overline{4}\ \overline{4}\ \overline{26}\qquad \overline{5}\ \overline{19}$

$\overline{24}\ \overline{19}$!

WHAT IS THE NAME OF THE
FEATHERS THAT GROW
ON A CHICKEN'S WING?

$\overline{1}$ $\overline{22}$ $\overline{24}$ $\overline{1}$ $\overline{26}$ $\overline{25}$ $\overline{20}$

$\overline{6}$ $\overline{25}$ $\overline{5}$ $\overline{19}$ $\overline{22}$ $\overline{25}$ $\overline{18}$ $\overline{7}$!

HENRY THE BUTCHER IS SIX FEET
TALL AND HAS BROWN HAIR.
WHAT DOES HE WEIGH?

$\overline{13}$ $\overline{25}$ $\overline{5}$ $\overline{19}$!

"IF I HAD A SLICE OF PIZZA
AND YOU HAD ONLY A BITE, WHAT
WOULD YOU DO?"

" $\overline{7}$ $\overline{1}$ $\overline{18}$ $\overline{5}$ $\overline{19}$ $\overline{1}$ $\overline{22}$

$\overline{24}$ $\overline{19}$!"

... More Coded Jokes and Riddles

A= 8B   N= 1D
B= 5D   O= 5E
C= 1B   P= 4B
D= 6E   Q= 2H
E= 4H   R= 6M
F= 7I   S= 5C
G= 2B   T= 7F
H= 9C   U= 3D
I= 8D   V= 2J
J= 2G   W= 6B
K= 3B   X= 3K
L= 9N   Y= 1G
M= 1D   Z= 7C

6B 9C 8B 7F

6E 5E

1G 5E 3D

1B 8B 9N 9N

8B

6E 8B 1D 1B 8D 1D 2B

5C 7F 4H 4H 6M ?

8B

5D 3D 9N 9N 4H 6M 8D 1D 8B !

88

WHAT DID THE PENCIL SAY TO THE
PAPER?

" ___   ___ ___ ___   ___ ___
   8D   6E 5E 7F   1D 1G

___ ___ ___ ___   ___ ___
4H 1G 4H 5C   5E 1D

___ ___ ___ ! "
1G 5E 3D

"DOES THE WATER ALWAYS COME
THROUGH THE ROOF OF YOUR CAR?"

" ___ ___ ___ ___   ___ ___ ___ ___
   5E 1D 9N 1G   6B 9C 4H 1D

___ ___   ___ ___ ___ ___ ___ ! "
8D 7F   6M 8B 8D 1D 5C

WHAT DID ONE POTATO CHIP SAY
TO THE OTHER?

" ___ ___ ___ ' ___   ___ ___
   9N 4H 7F   5C   2B 5E

___ ___ ___
7I 5E 6M

___   ___ ___ ___ . "
8B   6E 8D 4B

89

Find and circle the names of these endangered fish.

BONYTAIL   CHUB   CISCO
PIKE   PUPFISH   SQUAWFISH
STURGEON

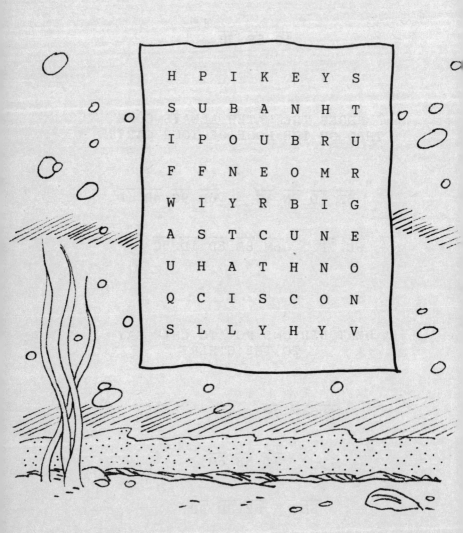

```
H  P  I  K  E  Y  S
S  U  B  A  N  H  T
I  P  O  U  B  R  U
F  F  N  E  O  M  R
W  I  Y  R  B  I  G
A  S  T  C  U  N  E
U  H  A  T  H  N  O
Q  C  I  S  C  O  N
S  L  L  Y  H  Y  V
```

There are two reasons why sea life is in danger.

To find out what they are, unscramble these words and place the numbered letters in their correct spaces below.

ISFH   __ __ __ __
                 4 12 6

TWERA   __ __ __ __ __
                    11   3

CNAOE   __ __ __ __ __
               1   7

LMMMAA   __ __ __ __ __ __
                        9

EILTPER   __ __ __ __ __ __ __
                8   5 10 2

__ V __ __ __ __ __ HI __ G   AND
1   2 3 4 5 6   7

__ O __ __ U __ __ ON .
8   9 10 11 12

91

Swamp deer make their home on the western slopes of the Himalayas. It is estimated that their population is dropping. There are two types of creatures, besides humans, that are responsible for their decrease in number. To discover the answer in the puzzle below, cross out all the odd-numbered letters and list the remaining letters, as they appear, in the spaces below.

3 F	4 T	17 X	12 I	9 I
13 T	5 E	14 G	2 E	5 F
8 R	10 S	7 S	15 F	6 L
7 V	4 E	4 O	12 P	1 N
2 A	6 R	9 M	22 D	18 S

__ __ __ __ __ __   AND

__ __ __ __ __ __ __ __

Find and circle the names of these endangered animals.

BISON   CHEETAH   SWAMP DEER   EAGLE

HYENA   JAGUAR   OCELOT   ORYX

OTTER   TAPIR   YAK

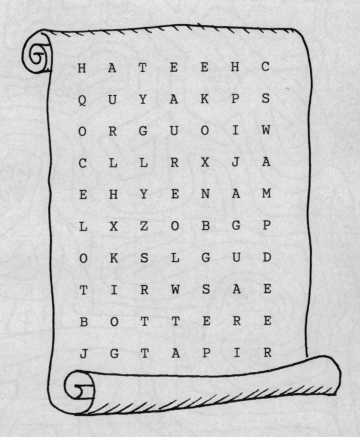

H A T E E H C
Q U Y A K P S
O R G U O I W
C L L R X J A
E H Y E N A M
L X Z O B G P
O K S L G U D
T I R W S A E
B O T T E R E
J G T A P I R

To get through this maze safely, you'll have to dodge the meteorites.

To travel correctly through this maze, follow
the path that spells SPACESHIP.

Guide the spaceship along the path of odd numbers.

This space creature doesn't know the alphabet. Help him through the maze by following the correct path, from A to Z.

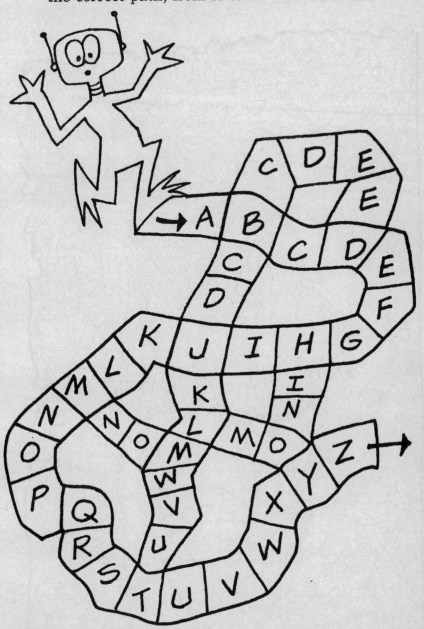

Find at least ten things that are different between these two pictures. Circle things on the next page.

Which three monsters are exactly the same?

Find and circle the listed things hidden in the
jungle scene.

Mouse	Wagon	Football
Telephone	Truck	Ostrich
Star	Hat	Balloon
Dog	Mitten	Bell
Kite	Turtle	Scarf

HOW YOU MOVE

In the following mystery word-search puzzle, find and circle the listed words. They can be found in straight lines going FORWARD, BACKWARD, UP, DOWN, or DIAGONALLY. Then, look at the remaining letters in the puzzle and use them to form the MYSTERY word.

BEND	CURL
CAPER	DANCE
CHARGE	FLUTTER
CREEP	HOP
	JERK
	JOG
	JUMP
	LEAP
	LUNGE
	LURCH
	PRANCE
	ROLL
	ROMP
	RUN
	RUSH
	SPEED
	STAGGER
	STOOP
	STROLL
	TWIST
	WALK
	WRITHE

MYSTERY WORD __ __ __ __ __ __ __

```
L L O R T S B E N D
U E L S T A G G E R
N A L O G R P E O R
G P O R A R P M U J
E P R H E S E S O E
A R C P D T H P T R
P A L A E L T S A K
O N N N R E I U L C
H C R U L W R A L L
E E C R T O W C P F
```

...Another Mystery Word-Search Puzzle

STATES

MYSTERY WORD ___ ___ ___ ___ ___ ___ ___ ___ ___ ___ ___ ___ ___ ___

ALABAMA	
CALIFORNIA	A A M A B A L A O C
DELAWARE	
CONN.	M I U K W N N I E O
IDAHO	M A N O R A H E I N
IOWA	
KANSAS	A A I R T O S R D N
MAINE	
MARYLAND	S T R N O S Y A E I
MASS.	S A O Y E F K W D M
MINN.	
MONTANA	H M S N L O I A E N
N. DAKOTA	
NEW YORK	D A N N T A H L N N
OHIO	S E T A A O N E A T
PENN.	
TENNESSEE	T A T U E K P D S C
UTAH	

103

PLACES TO SIT

MYSTERY WORD ___ ___ ___ ___ ___

H	B	E	N	C	H	R	D	S	R
S	I	L	L	O	H	I	O	I	U
B	I	G	R	C	V	A	A	C	G
D	L	S	H	A	Y	H	I	E	K
N	E	E	N	C	C	C	G	S	E
U	D	T	A	M	H	N	I	L	E
O	G	P	R	C	U	A	D	R	A
R	E	A	O	O	H	D	I	F	T
G	B	A	L	S	A	E	O	R	E
G	N	I	W	S	T	S	R	A	T

ARMCHAIR
BENCH
BLEACHER
CHAISE
DIVAN
GROUND
HIGH CHAIR
HORSE
LEDGE
LID
LOUNGE
MAT
POST
ROCK
RUG
SADDLE
SEDAN CHAIR
SILL
SLAB
SOFA
SWING
TRICYCLE

Another Mystery Word-Search Puzzle

FISH

ALBACORE
COD
DARTER
DRUM
GAR
GOBY
GROUPER
MARLIN
MINNOW
PIRANHA
RAINBOW
RAY
REMORA
SALMON
SHINER
SOLE
TARPON
TROUT
TUNA
TUNNY
WHITING

MYSTERY WORD — — — — — — — — —

```
S  W  D  A  R  T  E  R  O  A
Y  B  O  G  A  E  A  L  H  R
A  D  C  R  M  I  N  N  O  W
Y  L  P  R  N  A  A  I  H  S
N  O  B  B  E  R  R  I  H  R
N  O  O  A  I  P  T  L  E  S
U  W  M  P  C  I  U  M  I  A
T  Y  U  L  N  O  O  O  N  N
G  A  R  G  A  R  R  U  R  F
I  R  D  S  A  S  T  E  H  G
```

A Mystery Picture To Draw

This picture is a total mystery, but you can find out what it is. Draw exactly what you see in the numbered boxes at the top of the page into the blank boxes of the same number below.

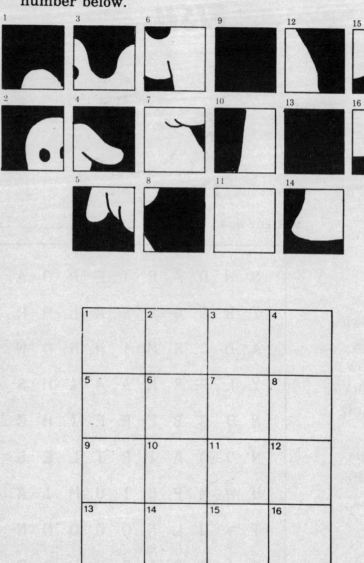

...Another Mystery Picture To Draw

... Another Mystery Picture To Draw

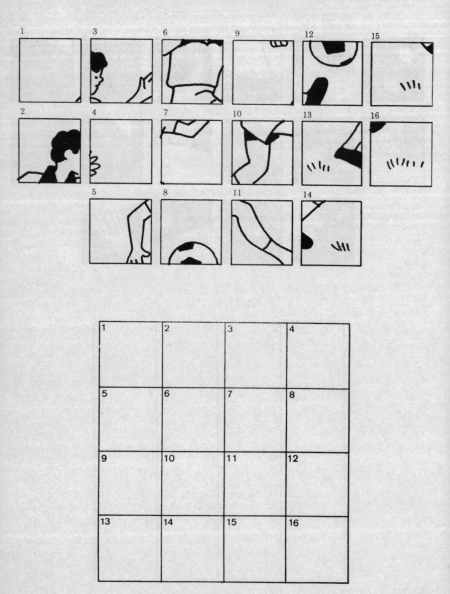

... Another Mystery Picture To Draw

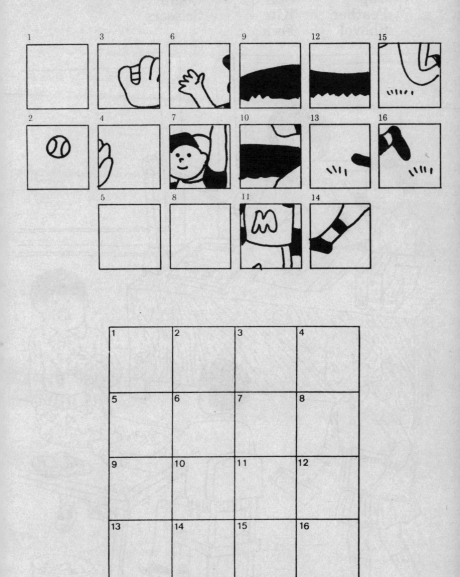

Find and circle the following objects hidden
in the picture below:

Cap	Star	Comb
Feather	Kite	Scissors
Shovel	Fork	

There is a message below, written in code numbers. To decode it, match the numbers with letters and write the letters in the blanks above the coded message.

A= 7   N= 24
B= 13   O= 12
C= 20   P= 9
D= 3   Q= 17
E= 16   R= 6
F= 2   S= 21
G= 8   T= 15
H= 5   U= 1
I= 10   V= 25
J= 26   W= 4
K= 19   X= 11
L= 23   Y= 22
M= 14   Z= 18

$\overline{}\;\overline{}\;'\;\overline{}$
$\underset{10}{}\;\underset{15}{}\quad\underset{21}{}$

$\overline{}\;\overline{}\;\overline{}\quad\overline{}\;\overline{}$
2 1 24   15 12

$\overline{}\;\overline{}\;\overline{}\;\overline{}\;\overline{}$
21 15 1 3 22

$\overline{}\;\overline{}\;\overline{}\;\overline{}$
4 10 15 5

$\overline{}\;\overline{}\;\overline{}\;\overline{}\;\overline{}\;\overline{}\;\overline{}$!
2 6 10 16 24 3 21

Find and circle the two stacks of books that are exactly the same.

Let's go to the cafeteria!
Can you unscramble these words
having to do with lunch?

I M K L   _ _ _ _

U F R T I   _ _ _ _ _

A E T M   _ _ _ _

O K C O I E   _ _ _ _ _ _

K N I R D   _ _ _ _ _

E S T A T   _ _ _ _ _

Double-Trouble Riddle Fun

In the following Double-Trouble puzzles, unscramble the underlined word in each riddle. Then find and circle it in the word-search puzzle on the opposite page.

1. When are swimmers like elephants?
   When they're wearing **KTRUNS**.

2. When is it dangerous to ride a cow?
   When its **HNORS** don't blow.

3. A book that is black and white should also be **DREA**.

4. What stays exactly knee high all year long?
   Your **EKEN**.

5. What kind of coat should you put on when it's wet?
   A coat of **NPAIT**.

6. Where was everybody during the big blackout?
   In the **RDAK**.

7. Nothing can be done to make a candle burn longer. Why?
   They all burn **SOHRTER**.

8. Why did the chicken go over the hill?
   Because it couldn't go **THGRUOH** it.

9. Why do cooks wear tall, white hats?
   To cover their **DHEAS**.

```
S T V M C U C H P
T H R O U G H A T
R E O R K A I N C
U A Z R S N R O H
N D Y E T C E D S
K S N A N E Y E E
S S C D D A R K K
```

WET PAINT

. . . Another Double-Trouble Puzzle

1. What kind of person loves cocoa?
    A **CCOOTUN**.

2. Why should ginger cookies be marked "FRAGILE"?
    Because ginger **NSAPS**.

3. When do crooks wear red suspenders?
    When they are **HUOPLD** men.

4. When is the only time it's polite to serve milk in a saucer?
    When you feed the **TCA**.

5. What's the proof that Santa Claus comes down chimneys?
    He is always covered with **ISUT**.

6. What's the secret of good health?
    Never get **KSCI**.

7. How did Captain Hook die?
    He scratched his **ENSO** with the wrong hand.

8. Why do birds perch in trees?
    They read the sign that said, "Keep Off the **SGSAR**."

9. What comes right up to the door but never comes in?
    The front **ESSPT**.

10. When is a highway like a skunk?
    When it has white **SITPERS** down its back.

11. When is a kid a magician?
    When he turns into a candy **ESTRO**.

```
S C E F G S H G
N O S E C N T R
U C N V A A S A
H O L D U P T S
H N S J U S R S
S U I T I L I T
R T L C E Y P E
T P K E S R E P
E M E R O T S S
```

1. What kind of water cannot be frozen?
   T H O water.

2. What did the father tree say to his son?
   You're certainly a **I C P H** off the old block.

3. What cap can be worn at the table?
   Your **E K N E** cap.

4. What did the boy squirrel say to the girl squirrel?
   I'm really going **T N U S** over you.

5. What has two hands but no arms?
   A **K C L O C**.

6. What would you call someone who is a sound sleeper?
   Someone who **S S O N R E**.

7. What kind of bulbs don't need soil or water?
   T L G H I bulbs.

8. What's the easiest way to tell the difference between a can of chicken soup and a can of tomato soup?
   Read the **B L E L A**.

9. What did the homeowner do when he got a big gas bill?
   He **E D P L X E O D**.

10. What did the woman say when she got a big phone bill?
    Who says talk is **P C E H A**?

```
P L C H E A P K J
C C C X X Z Y C G
L N S N P I H C N
O H I N L A B E L
C O O I O G P N C
K T G C D R T U B
K H K N E E E T L
T Y L O D E F S S
```

. . . Another Double-Trouble Puzzle

1. Why is it dangerous when ducks and geese stamp their feet?
   It can start an earth **Q K U C A**.

2. Why is it necessary to buy clothes?
   Because nobody gives them to us **E F R E**.

3. What can run but can't walk?
   E W R A T.

4. What do an engaged girl and a telephone have in common?
   They both have **G R S N I**.

5. What is the most important thing you should do every morning?
   You should **K W A E** up.

6. Why is it unsafe to put hair oil on your hair before taking a test?
   The answers might **P S L I** your mind.

7. What would you call a short-tempered apple?
   A **B C A R** apple.

8. What goes around the yard day and night but never moves?
   A **E F C N E**.

9. What knights-of-old rode camels?
   The Arabian **N S T I G H**.

10. What do an old car and a baby have in common?
    They both know how to **R T A T E L**.

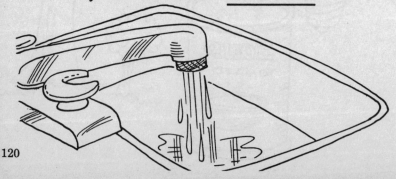

L R F E N C E
C R A B O R E
M W A T E R R
N I G H T S F
Q U A C K L U
C E K A W I E
R I N G S P F

Find and circle at least fifteen wacky things in this picture.

Find at least six things that are different between the "Video Pete" cartoon on this page and the one on the next page. Circle them on the next page.

"Search-a-Word."

In the following word-search puzzle, find and circle the words from the list below. They can be found in straight lines going FORWARD, BACKWARD, UP, or DOWN,

```
T B U D H Z T U E A H
C E G O D Z I L L A U
U A D C V N C D U H N
F S Y T L Y V K S A C
C T C O U H W W I R H
H W M R H Y D E N E B
A I N J T Y R R V P A
I T I E G S A E I O C
S H E K A I C W S E K
K F T Y M A U O I H O
S I S L E J L L B T F
Q V N L R K A F L F N
U E E U A L C V E O O
A F K L T E C D M M T
K I N G K O N G A O R
S N A Y O Y M U N T E
I G R M G U V N C N D
M E F M P B S F L A A
D R C U L A I G T H M
O S T M D S K V U P E
```

HERE COMES...

- DRACULA
- FRANKENSTEIN
- DOCTOR JEKYLL
- MR. HYDE
- MUMMY
- GODZILLA
- WEREWOLF
- KING KONG
- GAMERA
- HUNCHBACK OF NOTRE DAME
- BEAST WITH FIVE FINGERS
- INVISIBLE MAN
- PHANTOM OF THE OPERA

RIDE
WITH
A
WITCH

GHOST MANSION

```
T H G I R F S
C Y T S I M U
A K L W O H O
N A D D I M V
D E L T T A R
L R O B A L E
E C I O V S N
```

CANDLE · CREAK · DIM ·
FRIGHT · HOWL · LAB ·
MISTY · NERVOUS · OLD ·
RATTLE · SLAM · VOICE ·

WHAT HAPPENS TO SOME PEOPLE WHEN THE MOON IS FULL?

USE THIS CHART TO DECODE THE ANSWER.

A	B	C	D	E	F	G	H	I	J	K
12	8	14	23	20	21	24	1	26	7	25

L	M	N	O	P	Q	R	S	T	U	V
17	22	3	4	15	18	19	11	10	2	13

W	X	Y	Z
16	6	9	5

$\overline{10}$ $\overline{1}$ $\overline{20}$ $\overline{9}$

$\overline{10}$ $\overline{2}$ $\overline{19}$ $\overline{3}$

$\overline{26}$ $\overline{3}$ $\overline{10}$ $\overline{4}$

$\overline{16}$ $\overline{20}$ $\overline{19}$ $\overline{20}$ $\overline{16}$ $\overline{4}$ $\overline{17}$ $\overline{13}$ $\overline{20}$ $\overline{11}$!

MATCH UP

Which two pictures of The Eiffel Tower in Paris, France are exactly alike? Circle them.

LOOK AGAIN

Can you find at least six things that are different between these two pictures of the Statue of Liberty?

HORSE AND BUGGY

Where can you find horse and buggies like this still being used today? Fill in the areas that have a dot • to find out.

MIXED-UP LETTERS

Find these favorite vacation places in the letter jumble below.

- CALIFORNIA • FLORIDA • GEORGIA •
- HAWAII • MAINE • NEW YORK •
- PENNSYLVANIA • VIRGINIA •
- WASHINGTON D.C. •

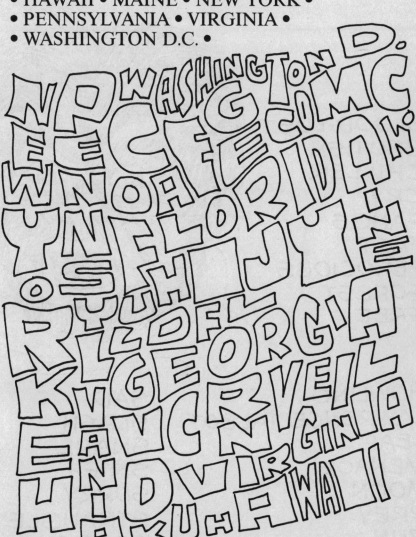

THE WOLF MAN

In the following SCARY word-search puzzles, find and circle the words from the lists. They can be found in straight lines going FORWARD, BACKWARD, UP, DOWN, or DIAGONALLY.

BLOOD-LUST
BRUTISH
CHILLER
CRY
FANGS
FAST
FEROCIOUS
FOREST
FREE

HOWLING
LAWRENCE TALBOT
LEAP
MENACE
MOON
PREY
RUN

SAD
SLASH
SNARL
SNIFF
SORRY
STRANGLE
WOLFISH

```
H O W L I N G T I
O S M E N A C E T T
S H A L L O L O O
T S U L D O O L B
R I T T S L S M L
A T N T N F N S A
N U L U A L I U T
G R D S R H F O E
L B T A L S F I C
E C R O S I O C N
O S G N A F R O E
P C H I L L E R R
Y R R O S O S E W
R E E R F W T F A
C S S Y T P A E L
```

THE MUMMY

ANCIENT
BANDAGES
CRYPTIC
CURSE
DRAG
EGYPTIAN
FOLKLORE
GORE
HIGH PRIEST
HORROR
HYPNOTIZE
LEGEND
MUSEUM
MYTH
OLD
SCROLL
SLOW
SNARL
STIFF
TOMB
VICTIM

```
C E R O L K L O F
M U S E U M D B L
T H F F I T S A F
S O W O L S N N A
E R M C V C D D N
I R O B I E F A A
R O L E C L E G I
P R N L T D S E T
H T Y M I L R S P
G O R E M O U A Y
I R L L O R C S G
H Y P N O T I Z E
L R D D N E G E L
C R Y P T I C D L
T L R A N S C L O
```

NIGHTMARES

ACTION
AWAKE
BED
CALL
CHASE
COLOR
DREAM
ESCAPE
EVIL
FALL
IMAGINATION
MONSTER
REACH
REAL
RUN
SCARE
SCREAM
SHAKE
SHOCK
SLEEP
SPOOKY
STARTLE
STRUGGLE
STUN
SWEAT
VICTIM
WEIRD

```
M E L T R A T S P
C O L O R C T S E
G N N O I T C A E
H U S S H A K E L
N S M I T C I V S
O U V S W E A T P
I D R E A M R N O
T R E N S U F U O
A I V C G A T T K
N E I G L L H S Y
I W L L A C B C K
G E S C A P E R C
A L A E R T D E O
M E R A C S E A H
I A W A K E E M S
```

FRANKENSTEIN

ABNORMAL
ASSISTANT
BLAZE
BOLTS
CASTLE
CRAZY
CREATE
CREATURE
CRYPT
DEAD
DOCTOR
ELECTRICITY
FEAR
FIRE
IT'S ALIVE
LAB
LIFE
MAD
OPERATE
SCARE
STALK
TALL
THUNDER
VICTOR

```
C F R E D N U H T
R E V I L A S T I
A O P E R A T E K
Z D R E T A E R C
Y A E Z A L B A K
T M K A T Y K C T
I K K S D E Y S N
C L A M R O N B A
I C I I L L L O T
R D F F A Y L L S
T O E B E C A T I
C C L K L A T S S
E T P T P Y R C S
L O V I C T O R A
E R U T A E R C P
```

A Mystery Picture To Draw

Copy exactly what you see in the numbered boxes from this page into the blank boxes of the same number on the next page. When you're finished, you'll find that something dangerous is swimming in the ocean's depths.

1	2	3	4	5	6
7	8	9	10	11	12
13	14	15	16	17	18
19	20	21	22	23	24
25	26	27	28	29	30
31	32	33	34	35	36

IT'S COMING RIGHT TOWARDS YOU!! WHAT IS IT?
CONNECT THE DOTS TO FIND OUT.

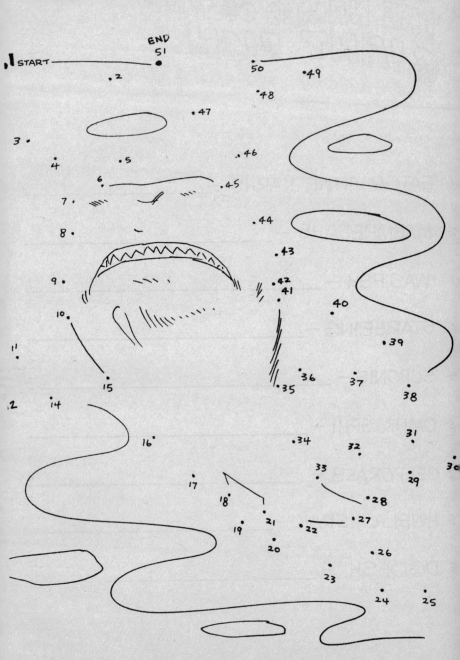

UNSCRAMBLE THE NAMES OF THESE GIANT FISH.

1- EATGR HITWE KARHS — _____

2- MAHMREDAHE — _____

3- WASIFSH — _____

4- STAREEING — _____

5- SUPONIF — _____

6- OMNK SFHI — _____

7- GELPORAEB — _____

8- HWELA HSRAK — _____

9- DGOFSHI — _____

A number of ghosts are passing by. Can you count them? Be careful. They're transparent, as most ghosts are.

In the scrambled-letter jumble on the next
page, find the frightening words listed below.

BATS
BLOOD
COFFIN
DEVIL
FULL MOON
GHOST
GHOUL
GOBLIN
HAUNTED MANSION
LIGHTNING
MONSTER
SCREAM
SHADOW
SKELETON
WITCH

AIIIEEEEEEE!

149

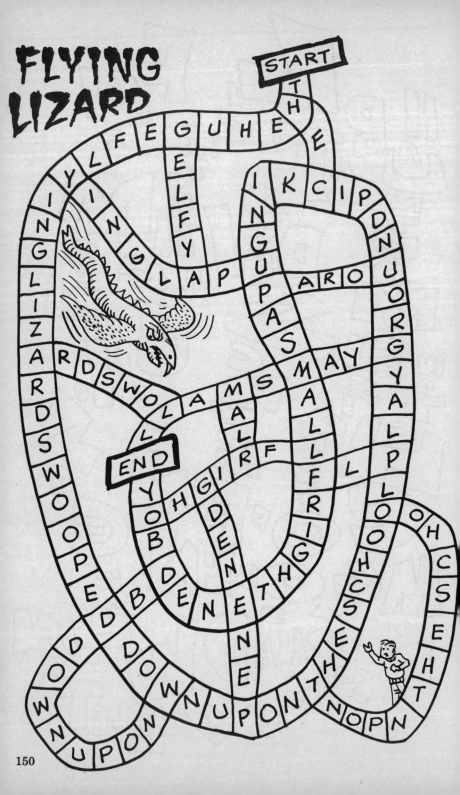

FLYING LIZARD

150

```
T H E G L U V B G J K T X Y M P
F U U C V I D N T N F R Z B O T
R G J G Y M N C L Y Z H B D Y X
I D T S E F L Y I N G Q R N N Z
G N G F R G H I Z Y U R Z U C Y
H T I C I Q P J A T C P X O N O
T C L D E N O K R K J G N R T U
E F P A Y U M L D V D C X G I G
N X I D E P O O W S T U C Y G C
E T C X T O W J U V E H L A T X
D G K O K N Y Z X T G T E L E T
C B I T X Z U P W O H L S P C N
D K N K L C A C K N D C D E E F
N P G W T O C J J T H S H X T S
G B S S V U D Y B O Y C B T B X
U I C U M W U V O B V U D W D Z
V N T Y C T L L A M S S O D I K
```

To get to the end of the maze on the left, you must find its scary message. Put the words from this message in the box below. Then, find and circle the words in the word-search puzzle above.

Find and circle the listed things hidden in the picture below.

Star	Pig	Fork
Ear	Block	Toothbrush
Log	Car	Santa
	Saw	Pipe
		Pie
		Eye

which 2 snowmen are the same?

CROSS-OUT PUZZLE

Cross out all the letters that appear **3 TIMES** in this diagram. Place the remaining letters, as they appear, in the blanks below. When you're finished, you'll find something fun to do in the snow.

A	B	J	S	K	M	C	L
M	O	A	P	E	K	Q	O
I	A	Q	U	J	V	Q	T
B	W	Y	G	X	B	V	C
F	■	T	■	H	O	■	N
K	R	J	F	C	X	N	Z
M	N	P	I	■	Y	Z	
P	D	■	T	F	■	W	Y
	Z	V	U	X	W	U	E

— — — — — — — — — — —

Cross out all the letters that appear **4 TIMES** and write the remaining letters, as they appear, in the blanks below. When you're finished, you'll be able to complete the message, "It's fun to go on a . . . ."

B	F	■	W	J	M	G	■	E
P	L	H	■	B	B	U	P	Q
U	V	F	U	J	M	Y	E	D
D	Z	M	F	A	H	G	P	Y
G	J	C	Y	H	A	E	■	G
Z	X	W	T	B	R	■	P	Q
D	I	Q	L	H	X	■	R	Z
U	Z	J	O	D	■	X	Y	■
E	■	R	L	Q	R	N	X	L
■	■	■	■	■	M	F	W	W

— — — — — — — —

Fill in the areas that have a dot • to see what came
out of the haunted house.

Fill in the areas that contain a letter from the word "ghost" to reveal a threatening scene!

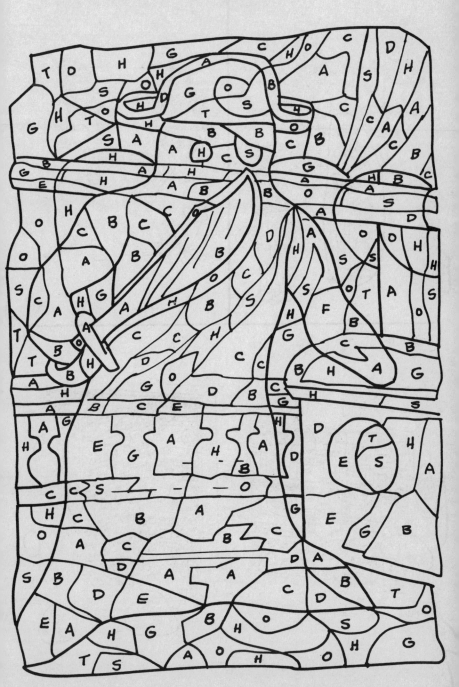

ANSWERS TO PUZZLES

Page 4

Page 5

Pages 6-7

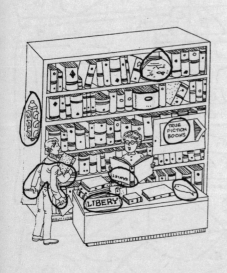

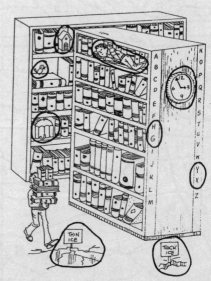

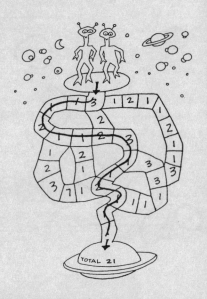

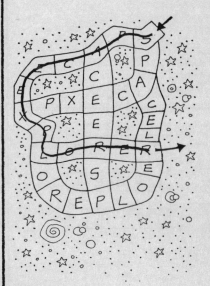

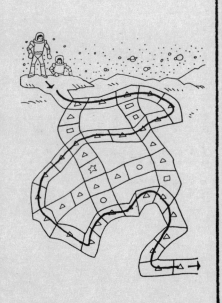

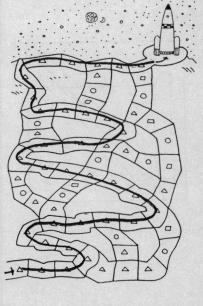

Page 12

```
 ¹M   ²E
³P O O L  L
 M    E
      V   ⁴M
      E   A
 ⁵S U N D A Y
 W        Y
 ⁶E I G H T
 E
 ⁷T R U E
```

Page 13

Page 14

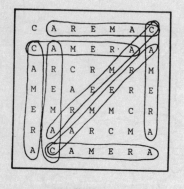

$$\frac{8}{\text{TOTAL}}$$

Page 15

SENDING

POSTCARDS LETS

YOU SHARE YOUR

VACATION WITH

OTHERS!

SPACE TALK

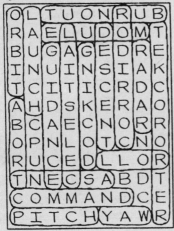

MOVING DAY

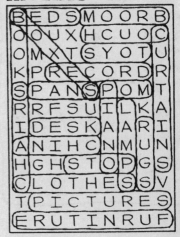

SUMMER

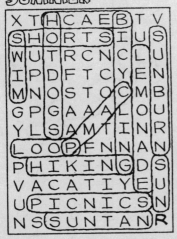

BREAKFAST

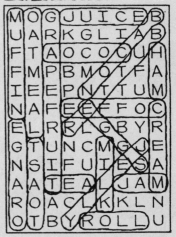

Page 20

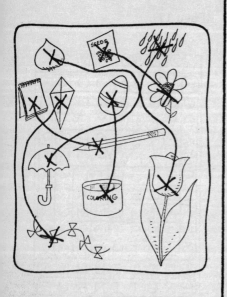

Page 21

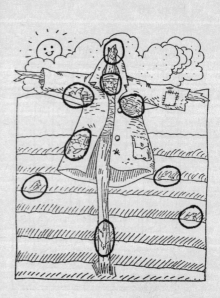

Page 22

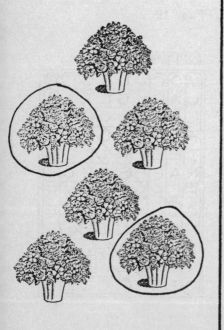

Page 23

SUN	MON	TUE	WED	THU	FRI	SAT
	1 L	2 N	3 H	4 B	5 Q	6 K
7 F	8 R	9 C	10 V	11 P	12 Z	13 E
14 A	15 M	16 U	17 G	18 W	19 J	20 X
21 I	22 T	23 O	24 Y	25 S	26 D	

W H A T   I S
THU WED SUN MON / SUN THU
18 3   14 22 / 21 25

A   B U L L
SUN / THU TUE MON MON
14 / 4   16 1   1

C A L L E D
TUE SUN MON MON SAT FRI
9   14 1   1   13 26

W H E N
THU WED SAT THU
18 3   13 2

H E   S
WED SAT / THU
3   13 / 25

S L E E P I N G ?
THU MON SAT SAT THU SUN TUE WED
25 1   13 13 18 21 2   17

A
SUN
14

B U L L D O Z E R .
THU TUE MON MON FRI TUE FRI SAT MON
4   16 1   1   26 23 12 13 8

WHAT GOES UP INTO THE AIR
WHITE AND COMES DOWN YELLOW
AND WHITE?

A N   E G G !
SUN TUE / SAT WED WED
14 2   / 13 17 17

WHAT DO YOU GET WHEN YOU
CROSS A KANGAROO WITH A
747 JET?

A   P L A N E
SUN / THU MON SUN TUE SAT
14 / 11 1   14 2   13

T H A T
MON WED SUN MON
22 3   14 22

M A K E S
MON SUN SAT SAT THU
15 14 6   13 25

S H O R T
THU WED TUE MON MON
25 3   23 8   22

H O P S !
WED TUE THU THU
3   23 11 25

A= •
B= ••
C= •••
D= |
E= ||
F= |||
G= −
H= ==
I= ≡
J= •|
K= •−
L= |•
M= −•

N= •|•
O= •−•
P= |•|
Q= −•−
R= •|••
S= ••|•
T= |−
U= −|
V= |=
W= =|
X= ||−
Y= −||
Z= ||=

W H Y
=| || −||

I S
≡ ••|•

T H E
|− == ||

S K Y
••|• •− −||

S O
••|• •−•

H I G H ?
== ≡ − ==

S O
••|• •−•

B I R D S
•• ≡ •|•• | ••|•

W O N ' T
=| •−• •|• |−

B U M P   T H E I R
•• −| −• |•| / |− == || ≡ •|••

H E A D S !
== || • | ••|•

"IF YOU SHOVELED SNOW FOR 25
PEOPLE AND THEY EACH PAID
YOU FOUR DOLLARS, WHAT
WOULD YOU GET?"

" A   N E W
  • / •|• || =|

B I C Y C L E !"
•• ≡ ••• −|| ••• |• ||

"IS THIS THE END OF THE LINE?"

" N O   I T S
  •|• •−• / ≡ |− ••|•

T H E
|− == ||

B E G I N N I N G
•• || − ≡ •|• •|• ≡ •|• −

A N D   W E · R E
• •|• | / =| || / •|•• ||

A L L
• |• |•

F A C I N G
||| • ••• ≡ •|• −

B A C K W A R D S ··
•• • ••• •− =| • •|•• | ••|•

Page 28

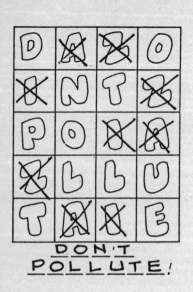

DON'T
POLLUTE!

Page 29

D O G S
6 8 12 11

A N D
13 16 6

C A T S
17 13 18 11

N E E D
16 20 20 6

L O V E
7 8 21 20

A N D
13 16 6

C A R E
17 13 22 20

Page 30

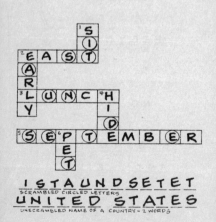

ISTAUNDSETET
SCRAMBLED CIRCLED LETTERS
UNITED STATES
UNSCRAMBLED NAME OF A COUNTRY - 2 WORDS

Page 31

164

Page 32

Page 33

Pages 34-35

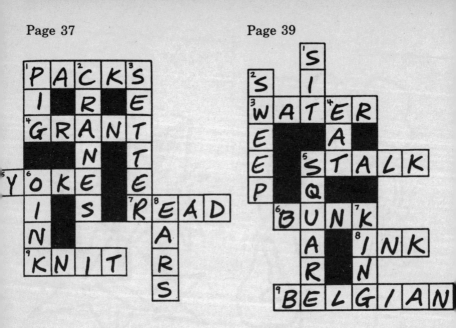

Page 37

Across: PACKS, GRANT, YOKE, READ, KNIT

Down: FIRE, ACORNS, KETTLE, TEARS

Page 39

Across: WATER, STALK, BUNK, INK, BELGIAN

Down: SIT, SWEEP, TEAR, SQUARE, KIN

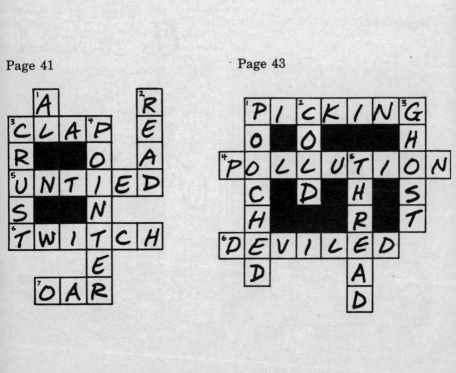

Page 41

Across: CLAP, READ, UNTIED, TWITCH, OAR

Down: A, CRUST, POINTER

Page 43

Across: PICKING, POLLUTION, DEVILED

Down: POACHED, HOSTS, TIDED, THREAD, GH

166

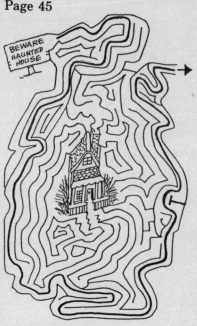

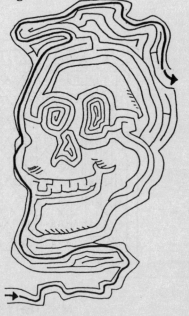

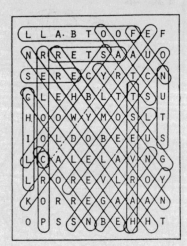

MYSTERY WORD   F R O S T

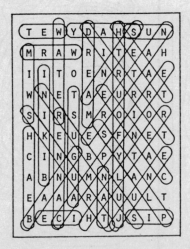

MYSTERY WORD   H O T

Page 50

```
G O N E
B           C
S   H       A
O   E       R
W I L D E L I F E
    E   P   E
    T   P
D E S T R O Y H
            O
            P
            E
```

Crossword letters:
- GONE
- OBSOLETE (B S O L E T E downward)
- HELP
- CARE
- WILDLIFE
- DESTROY
- HOPE

Page 51

DIBR	$\underline{B}\ \underline{I}\ \underline{R}\ \underline{D}$ 8
RNATUE	$\underline{N}\ \underline{A}\ \underline{T}\ \underline{U}\ \underline{R}\ \underline{E}$ 5
REHD	$\underline{H}\ \underline{E}\ \underline{R}\ \underline{D}$ 1 3
SILDERWNES	$\underline{W}\ \underline{I}\ \underline{L}\ \underline{D}\ \underline{E}\ \underline{R}\ \underline{N}\ \underline{E}\ \underline{S}\ \underline{S}$ 10 2 7
EMGIRAT	$\underline{M}\ \underline{I}\ \underline{G}\ \underline{R}\ \underline{A}\ \underline{T}\ \underline{E}$ 6 4 9

$$\underline{E}\ \underline{N}\ \underline{D}\ \underline{A}\ \underline{N}\ \underline{G}\ \underline{E}\ \underline{R}\ \underline{E}\ \underline{D}$$
1 2 3 4 5 6 7 8 9 10

Page 52

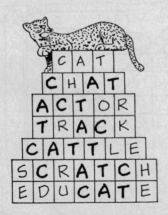

```
C A T
C H A T
A C T O R
T R A C K
C A T T L E
S C R A T C H
E D U C A T E
```

Page 53

```
⁵T  ¹⁰M  ¹¹D  ³H
⁷L  ¹⁵W  ¹O   ¹²B
⁴N  ²¹E  ⁸K   ¹⁰G
¹R  ¹⁶O  ¹L   ⁷V
¹I  ¹³Y  ¹⁸G  ²A
```

SOUTHWESTERN $\underline{M}\ \underline{O}\ \underline{N}\ \underline{G}\ \underline{O}\ \underline{L}\ \underline{I}\ \underline{A}$
2 8 4 10 12 18 6 2

169

Page 54

THAT'S ODD

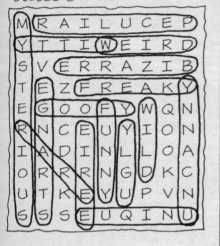

Page 55

BE A CLOWN

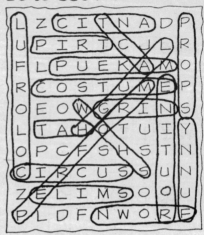

Page 56

WEIRD THINGS TO KEEP IN A CAR

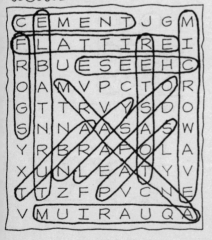

Page 57

WACKY SOUNDING "X" WORDS

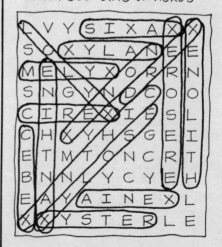

Page 58

Page 59

Page 60

Page 61

Pages 62-63

WHAT KIND OF MUSIC CAN BE PLAYED ON A SHOEHORN?

SOLE MUSIC!

WHAT KIND OF MUSIC DO MUMMIES DANCE TO?

RAGTIME!

WHAT KIND OF PETS MAKE MUSIC?

TRUMPETS!

WHICH FISH ARE THE BEST SINGERS?

BASS!

WHAT CAN'T BE BEATEN?

A BROKEN DRUM!

Pages 64-65

WHAT IS A MONSTER'S FAVORITE HOLIDAY?

APRIL GHOUL'S DAY!

WHAT HAS TEETH BUT CAN'T EAT?

A COMB!

WHERE WAS THE SPACE CREATURE WHEN THE LIGHTS WENT OUT?

IN THE DARK!

WHAT DOES THE MONTH OF DECEMBER HAVE THAT NO OTHER MONTH HAS?

THE LETTER "D"!

Pages 66-67

WHAT PART OF LONDON IS IN FRANCE?

THE LETTER "N"!

CHART CODE 21

WHAT KEEPS THE MOON IN PLACE?

ITS BEAMS!

WHAT PLANT HAS THE MOST MONEY?

MINT!

WHEN DID THE MILK BLUSH?

WHEN IT SAW THE SALAD DRESSING!

WHAT CAT IS FUZZY AND LOOKS LIKE A WORM?

CATERPILLAR!

Pages 68-69

WHY ARE ELEPHANTS SO POOR?

BECAUSE THEY WORK FOR PEANUTS!

WHERE CAN HAPPINESS AND MONEY BE FOUND?

DICTIONARY!

WHAT DO SNOWMEN PUT IN THEIR SALAD?

ICEBERG LETTUCE!

WHY CAN A HAMBURGER RUN A MILE IN UNDER THREE MINUTES?

BECAUSE ITS A FAST FOOD!

WHAT DO YOU CALL A SKELETON WITH NO BRAINS?

A BONEHEAD!

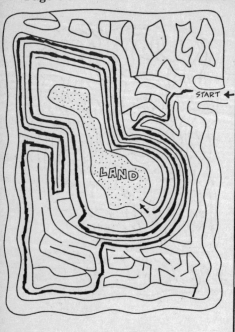

START ←

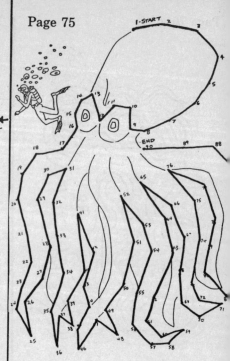

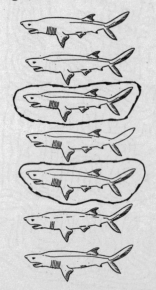

Page 78

U.F.O.'s ?

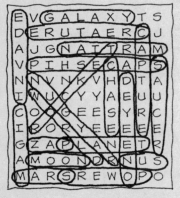

Page 79

YOU PUT PEANUT BUTTER ON WHAT ?!!

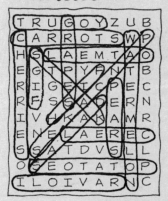

Page 80

30 WACKY THINGS TO BRING TO THE BEACH

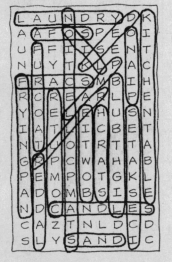

Page 81

WACKY PLACES TO HIDE MONEY

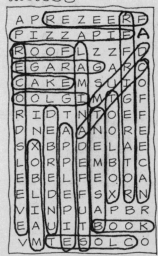

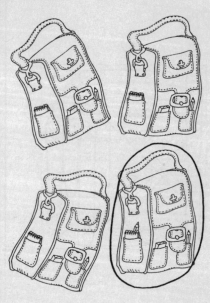

O B K O   <u>B O O K</u>
R D E A   <u>R E A D</u>
S L A C S   <u>C L A S S</u>
U B S   <u>B U S</u>
Y L A P   <u>P L A Y</u>
N R A E L   <u>L E A R N</u>

<u>H O M E W O R K</u>

A 5 B 11 C 1 D 10 E 25 F 6
G 12 H 22 I 24 J 23
K 26 L 2 M 13 N 20 O 4 P 21
Q 14 R 18 S 7 T 19
U 8 V 15 W 3 X 16 Y 9 Z 17

DOES YOUR
10 4 25 7 9 4 8 18

WATCH
3 5 19 1 22

TELL TIME?
19 25 2 2 19 24 13 25

NO, YOU
20 4 9 4 8

HAVE TO
22 5 15 25 19 4

LOOK AT
2 4 4 26 5 19

IT!
24 19

WHAT IS THE NAME OF THE
FEATHERS THAT GROW
ON A CHICKEN'S WING?

CHICKEN
1 22 24 1 26 25 20

FEATHERS!
6 25 5 19 22 25 18 7

HENRY THE BUTCHER IS SIX FEET
TALL AND HAS BROWN HAIR.
WHAT DOES HE WEIGH?

MEAT!
13 25 5 19

"IF I HAD A SLICE OF PIZZA
AND YOU HAD ONLY A BITE, WHAT
WOULD YOU DO?"

"SCRATCH
7 1 18 5 19 1 22

IT!"
24 19

A= 8B N= 1D
B= 5D O= 5E
C= 1B P= 4B
D= 6E Q= 2H
E= 4H R= 6M
F= 7I S= 5C
G= 2B T= 7F
H= 9C U= 3D
I= 8D V= 2J
J= 2G W= 6B
K= 3B X= 3K
L= 9N Y= 1G
M= 1D Z= 7C

WHAT
6B 9C 8B 7F

DO
6E 5E

YOU
1G 5E 3D

CALL
1B 8B 9N 9N

A
8B

DANCING
6E 8B 1D 1B 8D 1D 2B

STEER?
5C 7F 4H 4H 6M

A
8B

BULLERINA!
5D 3D 9N 9N 4H 6M 8D 1D 8B

WHAT DID THE PENCIL SAY TO THE
PAPER?

"I DOT MY
8D 6E 5E 7F 1D 1G

EYES ON
4H 1G 4H 5C 5E 1D

YOU!"
1G 5E 3D

"DOES THE WATER ALWAYS COME
THROUGH THE ROOF OF YOUR CAR?"

"ONLY WHEN
5E 1D 9N 1G 6B 9C 4H 1D

IT RAINS!"
8D 7F 6M 8B 8D 1D 5C

WHAT DID ONE POTATO CHIP SAY
TO THE OTHER?

"LET'S GO
9N 4H 7F 5C 2B 5E

FOR
7I 5E 6M

A DIP."
8B 6E 8D 4B

177

Page 90

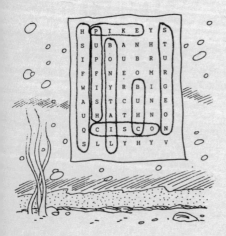

Page 91

ISFH $\underset{4}{F} I \underset{12}{S} \underset{6}{H}$

TWERA $W A T E \underset{11}{R}$

CNAOE $\underset{1}{O} C E A \underset{7}{N}$

LMMMAA $M A M M A \underset{9}{L}$

EILTPER $\underset{8}{R} E \underset{5}{P} T I \underset{10}{L} \underset{2}{E}$

$\underset{1}{O} \underset{2}{V} \underset{3}{E} \underset{4}{R} \underset{5}{F} \underset{6}{I} \underset{}{S}_{HI} \underset{7}{N}_{G}$ AND $\underset{8}{P} \underset{9}{O} \underset{10}{L} \underset{11}{L} \underset{}{U} \underset{12}{T} \underset{}{I}_{ON}.$

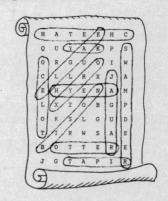

Page 92

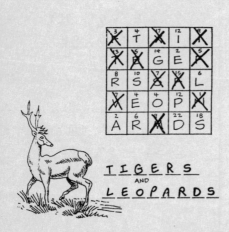

TIGERS
AND
LEOPARDS

Page 93

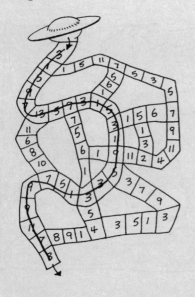

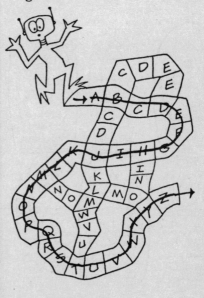

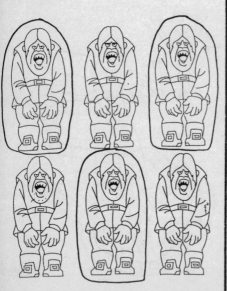

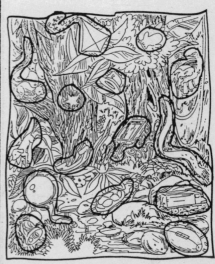

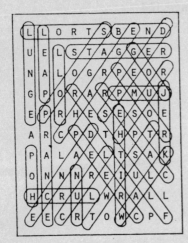

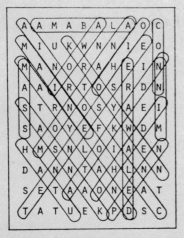

MYSTERY WORD G A L L O P

MYSTERY WORD

U N I T E D   S T A T E S

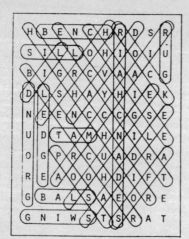

Page 104

MYSTERY WORD <u>S E A T</u>

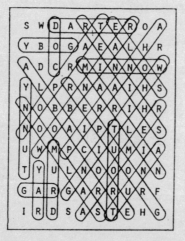

Page 105

MYSTERY WORD <u>S W O R D F I S H</u>

Page 106

Page 107

Page 108

Page 109

Page 110

Page 111

A= 7	N= 24
B= 13	O= 12
C= 20	P= 9
D= 3	Q= 17
E= 16	R= 6
F= 2	S= 21
G= 8	T= 15
H= 5	U= 1
I= 10	V= 25
J= 26	W= 4
K= 19	X= 11
L= 23	Y= 22
M= 14	Z= 18

$$\frac{I}{10}\frac{T}{15} . \frac{S}{21}$$

$$\frac{F}{2}\frac{U}{1}\frac{N}{24} \quad \frac{T}{15}\frac{O}{12}$$

$$\frac{S}{21}\frac{T}{15}\frac{U}{1}\frac{D}{3}\frac{Y}{22}$$

$$\frac{W}{4}\frac{I}{10}\frac{T}{15}\frac{H}{5}$$

$$\frac{F}{2}\frac{R}{6}\frac{I}{10}\frac{E}{16}\frac{N}{24}\frac{D}{3}\frac{S}{21} !$$

Page 112

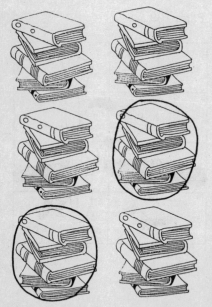

Page 113

I M K L	MILK
U F R T I	FRUIT
A E T M	MEAT
O K C O I E	COOKIE
K N I R D	DRINK
E S T A T	TASTE

Page 115

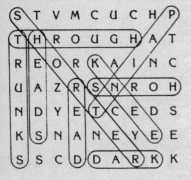

Page 117

Page 119

Page 121

Page 126

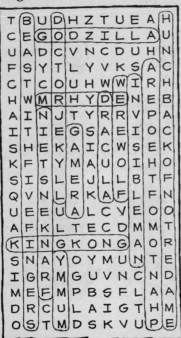

Page 127

Page 128

Page 129

THEY TURN INTO WEREWOLVES!

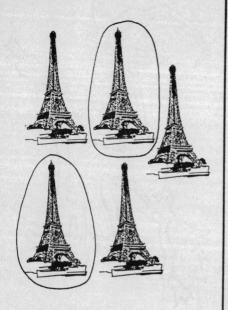

PENNSYLVANIA DUTCH AREA OF P.A.

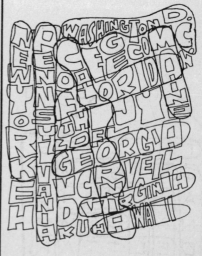

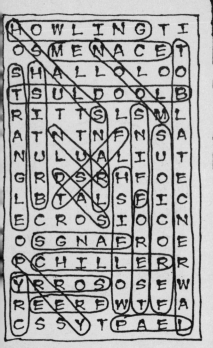

Page 135

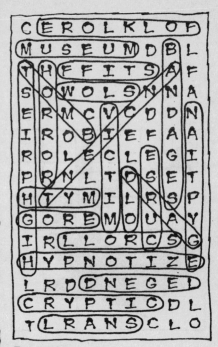

Page 137

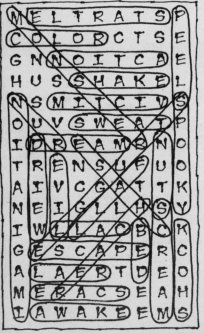

Page 139

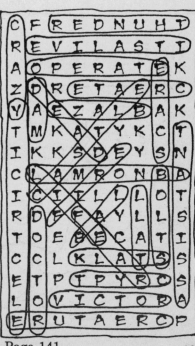

Page 141

Page 143

Page 144

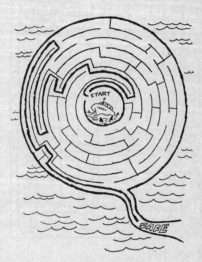

Page 145

Page 146

1. EATGR HITWE KARHS – GREAT WHITE SHARK

2. MAHMRE-DAHE – HAMMERHEAD

3. WASIFSH – SAWFISH

4. STAREEING – STINGAREE

5. SUPONIF – SOUPFIN

6. OMNK SFHI – MONK FISH

7. GELPORAEB – PORBEAGLE

8. HWELA HSRAK – WHALE SHARK

9. DGOFSHI – DOGFISH

11 GHOSTS

FLYING
LIZARD

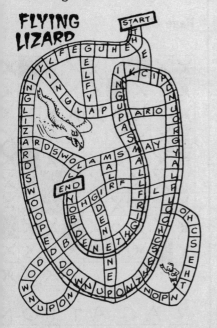

THE HUGE FLYING LIZARD
SWOOPED DOWN UPON
THE SCHOOL PLAYGROUND
PICKING UP A SMALL
FRIGHTENED BOY

Page 152

Page 153

Page 154

SLEIGH RIDE

Page 155

VACATION